12/96

WITHDRAWN

Gangsta

Gansta - by Ronin
Ro

Ronin Ro

Gangsta

Merchandizing the Rhymes of Violence

St. Martin's Press ⚹ New York

Portions of this book previously appeared in *The Source* and *Rap Pages*.

GANGSTA: MERCHANDIZING THE RHYMES OF VIOLENCE. Copyright © 1996 by Ronin Ro. All rights reserved. Printed in the United States of America. No part of this book may be used or reproduced in any manner whatsoever without written permission except in the case of brief quotations embodied in critical articles or reviews. For information, address St. Martin's Press, 175 Fifth Avenue, New York, N.Y. 10010.

Design by Pei Koay

Library of Congress Cataloging-in-Publication Data

Ro, Ronin.
    Gangsta : merchandizing the rhymes of violence / by
    Ronin Ro. — 1st ed.
        p.   cm.
    ISBN 0-312-14344-3
    1. Rap (Music) — History and criticism.   2. Hip-hop — United
States.   3. Gangs — United States.   4. Popular culture — United
States.   5. Music and society — United States.   I. Title.
ML3531.R6   1996
782.42164 — dc20   96-6951
                                                              CIP
                                                              MN

First Edition: July 1996

10   9   8   7   6   5   4   3   2   1

To Susan Deborah Young,

the woman I love

more than life itself:

Thank you for being there.

To the usual suspects

(Money Matt, Dynamite,

Michelob, Glen, Regan,

Jim and Rob Kenner):

Let's blow up the Earth!!!

To Cano, Vilma and

Santos Flores:

Much love to all.

To younger readers:

Stay in school,

not the streets.

And to all the real

hip-hoppers out there:

Keep reading!!!

Contents

Gangsta

Introduction: A Nation in Danger

1992: The skies are sunny and people are getting stabbed. Kid Frost walks through a mob of car enthusiasts who view the violence as a small annoyance. The gang scene is out of control. 'Bangers in various sets confirm that recent "riots" (said to protest the verdict in the Rodney King beating) were more gang-related than anything: some 'bangers admit that they saw the looting on TV and, bored, with nothing pressing on their schedule and in need of money, hurried to downtown's best stores before thieves stole everything.

The media pounces on the story: the right-wingers call it civil disobedience and attribute the looting to Black or Latino "criminals"; leftist magazines like *The Source* see it as political rebellion. Suddenly, dime-a-dozen gangsta rappers appear in *Rolling Stone*, with white writers indulging their liberalism and running half-page quotes from each. These non-skilled rappers believe their own press clippings and pat each other on the back.

I'm assigned this feature on Kid Frost, a figure on the fringe of hip-hop. In California, I immediately see that this will not be a clean-cut interview in a record label's conference room. I'm exposed to mad violence. I see how Frost is really living and how that reality away from the bright lights is buried in the lyrics on his album. Watching my back every minute, I jot down notes and sentence fragments. Surrounded by teenage killers and aging gangbangers, I feel out of my element like Fitzgerald's Nick Carraway, who only wants to say hello to his neighbor Gatsby but instead becomes sucked into a scene of booze, loose women, loud music and gangsters gone partly respectable.

At home in New York, I sit in bars, study my jagged notes and consider the puff piece *The Source* wants written. I realize that these Harvardite *Source* kids would rather use their pages to promote albums and stereotypes than to reveal the truth and urge their predominantly Black and Latino audience to pursue more positive paths. So I hand in my uncorrected notes. I become a household name in the hip-hop industry, receive more work from *The Source* (who now ride my dick and make me their "star writer") and I jump-start a rise in gang-related hip-hop articles. These bum-ass gangsta rappers always received their fair share of press ink but always about their sociopathic on-wax personas. With the Frost story, West Coast artists discovered a new marketing strategy: talk about your set and have a hip-hop journalist "riding shotgun."

Now, most hip-hop magazines tie artists to certain sets, and the gang and rap scenes are married when the two should cancel each other out: hip-hop was partly created in the South Bronx to counteract my birthplace's gang violence. But gangs and hip-hop become as tight as a wig and a bald head, and the hip-hop industry, already changed by NWA's record-breaking sales for *Straight Outta Compton, 100 Miles and Running* and *Niggaz4Life,* lives under the oppressive shadow of a handful of gangsta rappers with meager skills, drug-addled worldviews and far-reaching influence on American youth.

Before NWA's *Straight Outta Compton* album, hip-hop acts tried to steer youth in a more positive direction: Groups like Boogie Down Productions and Public Enemy told them to stop eating beef, to affect more natural hairstyles and to study their history; there were songs like "Stop the Violence," which urged kids to coexist in peace; and the hip-hop party was a unifying event filled with real MCs and not "rappers." A real MC (mic controller) says what they feel from the heart; they don't exploit sex and violence: they'll deliver good punch lines, insults, similes and metaphors. A "rapper" is an asshole who sits and concocts bull's-shit that will hit the pop chart or radio and make them rich; a "rapper" is more concerned with creating a catchy hook instead of dropping true lyrics.

Before NWA, we used to have more MCs and less rappers and all was right with the world. At these parties, white kids partied with Blacks and Latinos, straight partyers didn't bash gays, poor kids didn't rob their more affluent dance partners, urban youth didn't deride suburban, Jews didn't clash with Gentiles, and Korean grocers weren't demonized. Hip-hop was seen as a form that would inspire political change; we all believed that rap performers breaking barriers on shows like *American Bandstand* and *Soul Train*, and hearing our music in commercials for Polly-O String Cheese and Flintstones Fruity Pebbles was merely the first step to running the old folks out of office and replacing them with our political representatives, the Chuck Ds, Rakims and KRS-Ones. Rap albums were selling in the millions, MTV was kissing the rappers' asses, a worldwide audience formed and the music was filled with nothing but hope. Hip-hop would empower the inner city; we didn't see its perversion into the more "marketable" 'hood coming. We were going to be galvanized by art, not demonized.

In our own way, we were as idealistic as the hippies of the sixties, and we truly believed that everything would be all right; we would listen to our music, learn our history and unite to become a political force to be reckoned with. And we were on our way to becoming that just as NWA arrived to confirm the commercial viability of a strange new form of hip-hop.

For years, everyone credited Ice-T or KRS-One of Boogie Down Productions as the father of gangsta rap until KRS-One acceded that Schoolly D's "P.S.K." single (about Philadelphia's Park Side Killers gang) may have hit radio a second before BDP's *Criminal Minded* album. "Oh yeah, that did come first, right?" he said during a particularly grueling interview I conducted for *Spin*.

But, where Schoolly combined Run-DMC's prepackaged hardness with the explicitness of Slick Rick's "La-Di-Da-Di," KRS-One actually did produce the first true gangsta rap effort: instead of consciously fusing elements for effect, KRS' "9MM Goes Bang" touched upon events that Kris Parker actually grew up around, and it was a helluvalot more chilling.

From there, Ice-T abandoned his electropop roots and delivered his own Schoolly-like anthem, "6 in the Morning," which found an audience with those who were actually the victims of the LAPD's predawn drug raids. From there, Ice Cube wrote "Boyz-N-the 'Hood," another Schoolly-like work with Run-DMC–influenced deliveries, that recontextualized the East Coast b-boy aesthetic for West Coast gangland. Cube couldn't convincingly write about attending jams in violent New York nightspots like the Latin Quarter or Union Square or about bombing the Bronx-bound 4 train with sharp boxcutters at the ready, so he touched upon his immediate environment, the gang-plagued neighborhoods, drug-related shoot-outs and draconian op-pressiveness of the LAPD. By addressing these themes, he made one of the most primitive and profane rap albums ever recorded stand as the perfect encapsulation of a period in L.A.'s troubled history. Most importantly they delivered a work that moved Los Angeles rap past its embarrassing embryonic phase. Before NWA, the West Coast hip-hop scene was limited to exploitative Golan Globus films (*Breakin'* or *Rap-pin'*), "Planet Rock" knockoffs and bizarrely coiffed King Tut wannabes.

New York had the hardest groups (LL Cool J, Run-DMC, BDP, Big Daddy Kane); the comedians (Biz Markie, UTFO, Slick Rick); the political theorists (Public Enemy and Boogie Down Productions); the lyrical virtuosos (Rakim, Kool G Rap, KRS-One, Kane and Chuck D); and the trend-setting producers (Marley Marl, DJ Mark, Scott La Rock and the Bomb Squad). But *Straight Outta Compton* changed that: "The record not only put listeners within point-blank range of L.A. gang mentality, but it did so nonjudgmentally, without any sense of moral distance, going so far on some tracks as to use black-on-black violence as the metaphoric base for some of the group's boasting," as *Village Voice* writer Greg Tate pointed out.

By fusing the blue comedy of Redd Foxx, Dolemite and Richard Pryor to the urban grittiness of Iceberg Slim, then injecting the so-cial relevancy of Public Enemy and Boogie Down Productions, five bored Compton teenagers were able to go from religiously attending concerts by visiting New York groups Run-DMC and LL Cool J, to realizing their dreams of hip-hop stardom. *Straight Outta Compton* "shook the shit out of East Coast rappers and fans alike," wrote Tate, ushering in the era of gangsta rap and, most importantly, showing L.A. rappers that they too could sell a million copies to a built-in audience if they fashioned an image based upon the gang culture prevalent in California since the turn of the century.

As early as 1926, James Diego Vigil pointed out, there had been reports of a Mexican "boy gang problem" but local authorities thought they could contain the problem. They were sadly mistaken; older gang members began to indoctrinate their children into the culture, and it was these youth that grew to become the next generation, the 1940s pachuco gangs. Most of the gangsta fashion we see today in rap videos, in ads or on album covers can be traced back to these groups. The khakis on a Snoop Dogg were originally worn by pachucos whose older brothers fought in World War II; the tattoos on a Tupac Shakur were a prison influence on pachucos, as were the close-cropped haircuts and county suits. The Low Riders—old Chevrolets converted into works of Art by hardworking Mexican men—stemmed from the 1950s efforts by community officials and local authorities to divert youth from the influence of street gangs. They formed "car clubs," hoping that youth would spend time there instead of on the streets, but to no avail; the pachucos brought their ganglike attitudes and club titles to the organizations.

It was also the pachucos, still wary of whites after the media-created "Zoot Suit Riots," who introduced the concept of barrio pride and rivalries; they didn't want white thugs running into the neighborhoods (barrios) and randomly selecting Mexican-Americans for attack, so they united and guarded them from predatory outsiders (as opposed to modern 'bangers who see their barrios as " 'hoods," areas to control, intimidate and victimize).

When you see a young "gangsta rapper" on-screen, lighting up a joint while piloting a snazzy low-rider convertible on-screen, it's another tip of the hat to the pachucos, the generation of gangster that indulged in pro-social activities like partying and cruising. The pachuco era was followed by the 1960s "barrio warrior," who incorporated the nationalism of the emerging Chicano political movement and introduced the hairnets, bandannas and long hair that some gangsta rappers affect. By the 1970s, the Mexican gangsters were joined by their black counterparts, the Crips and Bloods and gang membership numbered in the thousands.

As many O.G.s (Original Gangsters who are older and survived to see this era) will point out, "gangbanging" back then meant riding the bus into someone's 'hood and mixing it up with the hands, bats, chains and maybe knives.

After 1980, however, cocaine was introduced and many gangs saw drug sales as a way of earning money; many sets (gangs) converted their neighborhoods into block-long drug spots and competition became as cutthroat as it was between stockbrokers on Wall Street. Guns were everywhere and gang members began living out Oliver Stone's screenplay for *Scarface;* the competition was murdered, Los Angeles became a war zone and the LAPD adopted fascistic methods in an effort to reduce the body count. Before NWA's *Straight Outta Compton,* however, the only examination of the culture could be found in Dennis Hopper's *Colors,* a pro-LAPD film that granted the Crips and the Bloods a national audience.

"At the beginning we point out that there are 250 men and women working in law enforcement against 600 gangs with over 70,000 members," a beleaguered Hopper told the *L.A. Times* in March of 1988, confirming that the gang problem was clearly not, as authorities in 1926 felt, something easily solved.

NWA figured that injecting gang-related topics, slang and fashions into their act would guarantee a built-in audience with the thousands of gang members infiltrating L.A., and they were right. But their album also struck a chord with white audiences bored with Run-DMC's tame heavy metal–styled anthems. With harder music and homicidal attitudes, as well as a hardcore fashion sense, which they later admitted stealing from Run-DMC, NWA upped the ante, became the band to beat and promoted the gangbanger ideology.

They were viewed as Leadbellies for a new age: they cursed and threatened anyone in their path, and they offered an alternative to merely being victimized by societal ills (as Melle Mel said he'd been, on Old School pioneer Grandmaster Flash's seminal "Message" of seven years before). Just as hip-hop's more positive acts were trying to steer the audience into nationalism, unity and political awareness, NWA's nihilism was set to more appealing music. The "positive" acts were viewed as anachronisms by a hyperprogressive audience and discarded while the one-dimensional gangstas signed six-figure album deals and dragged hip-hop away from its roots.

Gun homicide had been the leading cause of death for black teens since 1969, and while the mere presence of gangsta rap was not the sole cause of escalating murder rates, the casual attitudes that gangsta rappers exhibited while discussing Black on Black murder somehow made homicide acceptable. The music equated guns with masculinity, depicted them as "problem solvers" and stressed that, since other kids probably owned guns of their own, shouldn't we all be strapped?

Fourteen kids (age nineteen and under) will be killed in gun accidents, suicides, or homicides before sunset. (For this age group, the murder rate has increased 125 percent between 1984 and 1990.) Not even all natural diseases combined can equal the annual number of teenage deaths attributed to firearms. One out of every 28 Black males born is likely to be murdered; for whites, the ratio is one out of 164. If you're Black, the chances are higher of being murdered by one of your own: 1990 saw 93 percent of Black murder victims killed by other Blacks.

Although firearm homicide is still the number one cause of death for Black males aged fifteen to thirty-four, and the number two cause of death for all fifteen- to twenty-four-year-olds, a new handgun is still produced every twenty seconds. By the time you finish reading this paragraph, another gun will exist. Don't be fooled: death is random and senseless. There are more than two hundred million firearms in the hands of the American public (sixty-seven million of which are handguns). Those gun owners who religiously follow gangsta rap will have no compunctions about shooting. This is the only controversy surrounding gangsta rap—this, and whether these primitive rappers deserve to have record deals; because rap can be a "Black CNN" and a "voice of the disenfranchised diaspora" and all of that other shit, but first and foremost, it's a form of entertainment. If gangsta rappers have to rely on this shock-value bullshit for attention, then maybe they don't have any talent and the status of their record deals should be reevaluated.

 nstead of urging listeners to "fight the power" or improve their community, as Boogie Down Productions and Public Enemy had done, gangsta rap told listeners to direct their anger against their own kind. And soon, as they had done when the nationalists topped the sales charts, the audience began to listen. Whereas P.E. and BDP helped wean youth off of the addictive habits of gold jewelry, self-hate and straightened hair, gangsta rap influenced youth to buy guns and adopt a paranoid victim's worldview.

While the mainstream media haggled over censorship issues surrounding the music, the gangsta rappers began translating their on-wax fantasies into full-scale reality. Many were soon entangled in legal problems and shootouts, and their listeners grew further entranced. Soon, the listener—young, lacking role models or authority figures, and somewhat bored with life—would accept the gangsta rapper's lyrics as gospel.

What's most shameful is the East Coast reaction to the string of platinum albums streaming from the West Coast. At first, certain East Coast artists vehemently denounced gangsta rap's regressive attitudes, and tried to counteract them with positive, socially conscious albums; but when these albums failed to match the million-plus sales of a Too $hort or a DJ Quik, they rethought their philanthropy and began injecting gangsta elements into their verse.

Another extreme East Coast reaction came from artists like Tim Dog, who tried building careers around attacking West Coast rap with the same style and attitude. By substituting South Bronx housing projects for Compton 'hoods and describing the very same scenarios, artists like Tim hoped to garner platinum sales. The apotheosis arrived when Kool G Rap, once known for lyrical intricacy, enlisted Ice Cube's producers and simplified his style, hoping to produce a platinum-selling work, and when the group Onyx fashioned their own gangsta rap persona and tried to popularize a new subgenre called "horror-core." Horror-core was to hip-hop what death metal is to Brahms or Mozart. Now the East Coast hip-hop scene is rife with death-obsessed groups like the Gravediggers or the Flatlinerz, with the drug culture chic of artists like Biggie Smalls and Fat Joe, with trigger-happy acts like Smif-N-Wessun and M.O.P. and with Snoop impersonators of every shape and size.

With New York groups incorporating gangsta elements, the West Coast continuing to generate million-dollar sales and the Midwest sounding like NWA circa 1988, the formerly marginal strains of gangsta rap, now set to ParliaFunkadelicized grooves, have come to define hip-hop as a whole. And it's fast on its way to casting its shadow—projecting the artists' drug abuse, misogyny and self-hate—over this generation.

That gangsta rap has grown so large may explain why white kids now affect gangbanger fashions and attitudes in Little Rock, Arkansas; it may shed light on why murder figures are rising in low-income areas; antisociality is now the norm, and the gun, and not mediation, is the primary arbiter of social conflict.

With *Gangsta*, a collection of nonfiction articles I've written over the years, I've tried to examine the music, its personalities, and the influence it holds over American youth. I've tried to explain how, when gangsta rap became the Next Big Thing and record labels inundated the market with NWA clones, the music changed—and with it, the mentality of the next generation.

Some people say this is Generation X, and for some white folks subsisting on fast-food paychecks, it may be; but for the majority of Americans—of all colors, income brackets, races and creeds—this is the age of the The Gangsta. Simply glance at the murders reported in your newspaper's local section and you'll see how the drive-bys and jackings mentioned by NWA years ago have become a full-scale reality, to the point where these quaint slang terms have now been incorporated into the English language.

Almost every state in the union has a Crip or Blood or Crip/Blood–styled gang wreaking havoc, and some of the gangs are white and Asian. Children have lost respect for authority figures; fatalism informs their minds and they express themselves through violent acts. And those of us over twenty-five have come to have a healthy fear of teenagers: not because they dress in a shocking manner or listen to loud music, but because we know that some of these teens won't think twice about pulling out an illegal handgun and ending a life. So many kids—well-read and smarter than you'd imagine—have adopted the gangsta mentality as a rule for living: "Do or Die." Law enforcement agencies can buy more vests, build more prisons and rework the Constitution all they want, but no steel-versus-steel approach, gun-control law or "Three-Time Loser" crime bill will change the opinions of this damaged generation.

Until record companies realize that this music is directly impacting the quality of American life, and stop quoting "Constitutional free speech" bullshit simply to protect their financial concerns—and when they stop signing violent groups and promote positive acts—only then will gangsta rap, marketed from its inception as "street reality," release the stranglehold it has on the national psyche. Because it's not only this generation being affected. Once you see your dyslexic ten-year-old nephew misspelling words and having trouble reading, but effortlessly quoting Snoop Doggy Dogg's verse from "Ain't Nuthin' But a G-Thang," you may come to have a better understanding of how gangsta rap is transforming the American character.

Gangsta is not an anti–gangsta rap tract, nor is it a defense for "ghetto griots" (as inept writers once called them). It's a call for all involved to wake up and accept responsibility for their part in what has become a national tragedy. It's about a retrogressive music destroying a form of expression that once unified people. It's about gangsta rap's effect on everyone in the hip-hop industry, and how horrific elements from the music and videos creep slowly into reality. Since this perversion of hip-hop shows no signs of fading away, I humbly submit this work in hopes that it will reach artists, the media and, most importantly, our young.

Inside these pages, you'll read about artists who record the music and ensure its survival (Kid Frost, South Central Cartel, Dr. Dre and Snoop, Scarface, Cypress Hill) and the artists who denounce it (Mellow Man Ace, A Lighter Shade of Brown, the 2 Live Crew). You'll read about artists who incorporate gangsta elements in their music for lucrative West Coast sales (Method Man, Naughty By Nature, Street Mentality) and artists who struggle against the genre (Whodini, Gang Starr). You'll read about artists who discover that their music has changed the American landscape (Too $hort and the Dangerous Music Crew) and those artists who lived a larger-than-life lifestyle but regretted it when faced with the sobering reality of early death (NWA founder Eazy-E). You'll read about the influence it has on youth in Tokyo, who wear khakis and Raiders jackets, or how local Crips in Atlanta wave gang signs and engage in drug-related shoot-outs; how robbery gangs in Brooklyn, New York, will strip you of your Ralph Lauren clothes while mouthing lyrics by Gang Starr or Wu-Tang Clan. You'll see how the music has told any average kid in any American city or suburb in the 1990s that the best way to end a problem is to shoot it.

Hopefully, *Gangsta* will show any aspiring gangbanger, gangsta rapper or garden-variety juvenile delinquent that, as Cypress Hill's Sen Dog said, "being someone in this life is easier than you think." Hopefully it will dispel some of the more glamorous myths that have come to surround the culture after Dennis Hopper's *Colors*, John Singleton's *Boyz N the Hood*, and the Hughes brothers' *Menace II Society* helped change gangsters into folk heroes.

Though there are many disparate stories and personalities in *Gangsta*, the stories are connected. In each, the artists exist in the shadow of gangsta rap, and most of their difficulties are due to the music or to the behavior it inspires or encourages among its audience. *Gangsta* may not feature chapters on your favorite break-dancers, graffiti artists or Old School veterans, but it's still a hip-hop book. It details the regression of the art form into a minstrel show, where performers battle over who drinks more 40s, kills more niggaz, jacks more cars, slaps more hoes, and emerges as Gangsta Degenerate #1. It may not drown you with statistics but it's social science of a sort: root causes behind societal violence and pathology are included but not in the usual dry, egghead manner.

Gangsta is a sad book; also funny, entertaining, enlightening, but most importantly, life-affirming. Through the stories, the reader will be able to trace the changes in hip-hop and in American youth. It begins in 1992 as gangsta rap rises to prominence, and ends three years later, when the scene is dominated by it and East Coast artists return to intricate styles in an effort to reclaim a once proud, time-honored position. I've written in a way that suggests fiction, but every word is true: the artists don't lead storybook lives; the labels don't love them; gangsta rap is destroying hip-hop; gang members are an unwanted minority in decent communities; and modern American stories rarely have happy endings. Hopefully, this will be the book that readers turn to for an overview of our troubled times, accomplishing for hip-hop what F. Scott Fitzgerald's works accomplished for the Jazz Age.

April 1995
Ronin Ro
Brooklyn, New York

Chapter 1

Riding Shotgun

The checkered blue-and-yellow taxicab cruised past pastel-toned buildings, two to three stories high, while the egregious sun filled the backseat with harsh light. To my left, outside of the passenger window, Maximas and hatchbacks. Studying them, I considered rumors I'd heard about Los Angeles: there were supposedly "freeway killings," where someone in the next lane would catch you staring, pull a pistol and blast. Sighing, I nervously inhaled on my cigarette and watched a green sign reading LOS ANGELES: EAST whiz by.

According to Kid Frost's records, East L.A. was a war zone, brimming with pro-violent cholos who shot anyone wearing blue or red. The cab swerved off of a freeway exit, twisting onto a four-lane street sandwiched by fast-food drive-thrus and gas stations, and the driver — a gray-haired Mexican man of indeterminate age — half turned.

"First time here?" he asked.

Wanting to avoid the costly "scenic route," I grunted like a veteran, reclining on the seat, blew smoke out of my open window and examined the landscape: the bland colorless streets, the swinging palms, the hills, buildings and the indigent. I felt green as an apple, and did not trust this driver. Visions of him driving along, passing the hotel. "Hey, that was it, right?" Pulling to a stop near an abandoned railroad. With gun in hand, "Gimme all your . . ." Good Lord, the drinking was rotting my mind.

To relax, I retreated into thoughts of that rainy morning in New

York. Scurrying to catch a cab, I bumped into a female friend I'd always wanted to sleep with. A mere five hours later, and I was in 75-degree sunshine, my hooded sweatshirt suffocating me and my next to last cigarette burning quickly.

I met Kid Frost once in New York, at a *Wild Style* party in Ninety-seventh Street Park. That summer afternoon, hip-hop groups were boycotting The New Music Seminar. Son of Bazerk and Just Ice were out there; Grandmaster Flash and Biz Markie; members of the ColdCrush Brothers and the Rock Steady Crew; and a documentary film crew of which I was a part.

As Frost, who was dressed in a light-blue county shirt and dark-blue denim jeans, stepped in front of the camera, his boys circled like malevolent disciples. The cameras rolled and I asked him questions but the "interview" was more like Frost rambling on for fifteen minutes. The thirty-five millimeter film recording this was expensive, but Frost, enamored with his own voice, continued ranting. My girl at the time, a busty dimwit named Anna, clapped her hands in delight. "Ooh!" this ardent Frost fan cooed. "I just love that song 'La Raza,'" she added, eyeing his porky frame with prurient interest. Infuriated, I skipped questions and tried to save film.

As the cab cruised towards Rodeo Drive, I wondered why, one month after dissing Frost's album in *The Source* review section, I accepted this assignment. At the time, the schmucks at *The Source* wouldn't let me write features. Until Jon Shecter called. "How would you like to write a feature?" I said I wanted to cover Public Enemy. "Just do your Kid Frost story for 'La Raza,'" he laughed.

"But no one wants to read about this guy!" I countered. "Nobody likes his shit!"

"Frost has a large regional audience in parts of Texas," I was told. What would I write about? I thought; Frost's whole "Mexican Chuck D" schtick? I'd heard enough from this windbag during our "interview."

But the cab continued its journey, passing a park where ponytailed white men and shit-assed earth-mother types were holding a pottery art fair barely three weeks after the Rodney King riots. And these bag-toting, three-bean-salad-eatin' white bastards were already back to buying jewelry and sportswear on Rodeo, then browsing at Mexican-styled arts and crafts. On West Hollywood's palm-covered streets,

Gangsta: Merchandising the Rhymes of Violence

bleary-eyed Mexican men waited at bus stops near Rolex-wearing whites in European luxury cars. A huge, year-model Jeep rolled by, crammed with blondes in baseball hats, bikini tops and sunglasses, searching, it seemed, for some ethnic dick or some "minority" to sell them drugs.

We drove on, past the gleaming business towers Michael Crichton would say were bought up by faceless Japanese businessmen during the 80s, and entered a more urban stretch of town. More urban because its walls were covered with archaic tags, and LAPD squad cars crept down these poorer streets, mad-dogging pedestrians and peering into windows of passing cars.

Soon, we arrived at the hotel. I brushed past Mexican bellhops and cardboard whites in sober gray Brooks Brothers. At the front desk, a young black woman with gold fronts handed me a key card. In my room, I switched on the TV and studied the KCBS local news: a Victims of Crime program had been unveiled to assist city residents victimized by the recent riots; Stacey Koon, one of the officers acquitted of battering Rodney King, discussed the new book he was publishing (which featured racial slurs); the brother of one of the L.A.4 (accused of the Reginald Denny answer-back beating) organized a press conference on the front lawn of his home in South Central; big-city mayors (including New York's David Dinkins) held hands and marched down a Washington, D.C., street; last night, someone fired three shots into a passing police car in downtown L.A., and missed; a new designate police commissioner, Willie Williams, was being flown in from Philadelphia; and real-estate values were down.

■■

From his independent-label collaborations with Ice-T to *Hispanic Causing Panic*, he had always offered himself as a spokesperson for Chicanos in the 'hood. Best remembered for "La Raza," he urged Chicano gangs to unite, then set out to organize the Latin Alliance, a collective of rappers that included Mellow Man Ace (of "Mentirosa" fame) and ALT (a French-Mexican rapper who had ghostwritten Frost's more-known songs). The supergroup would record an album, cover War's "Low Rider," a staple of the low-rider car culture, and see the update become a regional megahit! After a colorful video—all smiles and tough talk—they vanished from sight.

No one knew The Alliance had disbanded until Mellow Man Ace, in Manhattan to promote the Brother With Two Tongues, said: "The Alliance broke down like an appliance." Frost, he explained, was bringing that "cholo shit into hip-hop and everybody out here ain't down with that shit." In addition, Frost had "banned" Mellow from appearing at live gigs, so as to not pay him his cut, Mellow claimed. "He's walking around with a swelled head and nobody wants to be with him. If you're coming out to L.A. we'll kick it."

After my arrival in Los Angeles, Mellow walked ahead of me. Clad in loose T-shirt and baggy pants, a far cry from the elegant white suit on his latest album cover, he approached a row of parked cars in front of the small 38 Fresh Recording Studio.

A Lighter Shade of Brown—ODM and DTTX, a local duo known for their saccharine oldies updates—stood out front. ALT, a reserved young man with a fiendish goatee, dressed in East Coast fashion, emerged from the studio and said "W'sup" to everybody. "I'm just finishing this remix for my album." After one or two questions ("You from New York, vato? Is it as crazy as we hear?"), everyone began relating horror stories about Frost.

First: the incident on the set of *Pump It Up*.

"We got there and 'The Man' was sitting there with his kid and his guards," said DTTX, treating Frost's name as one would a spell that conjured demons. "We just walked in and said 'W'sup' and started shooting pool. Then The Man walks up to Mellow and said, 'This shit has gotta stop! You don't be bringing punks I'm mad at around here.' Mellow told him straight up, 'Fuck you, these are my homies! I'm'a bring whoever the fuck I want. I'm on this show too! Not just you!' Frost said, 'Just come outside and we'll take care of it. I don't wanna fight in front of my kid.' The Man's what? Twenty-eight years old? Picking on kids like us? I'm only eighteen!"

Frightened and more than a little disillusioned, DTTX couldn't understand why his former idol could want to brawl with kids who bought his records. Forehead creased with worry lines, D sounded persecuted. "Frost asked me to square up with him," said Mellow, "but he picked up a cue stick and came at me!"

"I guess Mellow just said 'Fuck that!' " OMD quipped: "He started yelling, 'You wanna fight?! You wanna fight?!' "

The run-in was the origin of the war of words playing itself out in various hip-hop magazines.

While angry, Lighter Shade clearly avoided saying too much about what they perceived as other people's problems. It was best to stay shut and let the others fight it out themselves.

When airing a grievance, they prefaced it with declarations of respect for Frost and his music, "which we do enjoy!" Their beef started after they secured a deal with independent-label Quality Records. Able to meet their hero, they cultivated an industry, hi-and-bye friendship. While at a radio interview, a group member accidentally said, "And this one's by Kid Frost," over a song by pop-rapper Gerardo, which used a similar sample. Frost heard about the error and got it into his head that these sniveling little shits were trying to equate his hardcore political music with mindless crossover pap. Unaware that Frost was offended, Lighter Shade crossed a post-concert party to shake his hand, only to discover they were topping the Kid Frost Shit List! "Hey, Frost, w'sup!" "Fuck that! You dissed me!"

"In Texas and other places, wherever we went, people were coming up and asking if we were cool with Frost," OMD explained: "They were telling us about how he was dissing!" During his sets, Frost would interrupt songs to lead the crowd in "No justice, no peace"–like chants against Lighter Shade. "They're sellouts to the Mexican culture," Frost would say, playing the race card and anything else ("They're going pop!") that he could against what he considered the Gruesome Twosome.

"It seems that Kid Frost is at war with other rappers . . ."

"Particularly Latinos . . ."

■■■

Sunday started with uncharacteristically gray skies and a light drizzle. UP FROM THE ASHES, L.A. GETS DOWN TO WORK, read the headline to the *West Hollywood Independent*. Kid Frost seemed a bit paranoid, and I'd have to face him. I'd written a negative review of his latest album, which had seen print in *The Source*'s infamous TLC issue. A rented car, driven by a blonde named Alison, passed the hills where Charlie Manson and his band of drifters slaughtered the pregnant Sharon Tate. "He lives in Van Nuys?" Alison asked rhetorically: "A lot of studio people live there. But there's also Hispanics! The area's changing. . . ."

As we reached his home, the sun broke through the clouds. Round, with squat legs and muscular arms, in plaid shirt, khakis and black shoes, Frost appeared; strolling down a long driveway, unlocking the gate surrounding his estate, impatiently waving his hand, and admitting us into his world. After locking the gate, and us inside, he walked past the car. A Dalmatian and a pit bull roamed the grounds. His son Elijah shadowed his father. On the stoop of the modest home sat Block, one of Frost's boys, loading a small 380. "You the guy from *The Source*? This is the guy?"

Frost nodded then officially welcomed me. "That review of my album was fucked up. You wrote it and I could be real upset," he nodded, glancing quickly at Block, who now loaded bullets into clips. "I figure you don't know what the fuck you're talking about: the culture or the slang. That's why I want you to come with me to the car show."

Walking into his music room (a converted bedroom filled with equipment turntables, records and clippings from *Low Rider* magazine), Frost's moptopped son nodded his head to a beat his father tapped out on a Roland 808 drum machine. "People like NWA are talking about things they don't know from experience. That whole look with the jail clothes and khaki pants? That's a Chicano thing. You can see it in the beginning of *Chico and the Man*, back in the seventies when they filmed that Mexican dressing like that." Reclining in a chair in front of a mixing board, Frost denigrated the recurrent motifs in West Coast hip-hop: shooting niggas, smacking hoes, slanging keys. "That's the kind of shit that people do as fantasy and other people hear and make reality. It's irresponsible, dude."

Outside, by his swimming pool he raised the 380, eyed a nearby tree, then squeezed off: emptying a full clip in seconds. Every bullet, he proudly noted, had struck its intended target. His son, right behind him, agreed. "This got viscosity," he told Block, strolling past us. "You see that shit? My neighbors all know me. They know I bust caps. And no police come either. I can kill somebody out here."

"Bury them in the yard," Block chuckled.

In his garage, he displayed his gleaming white 1964 Impala. "A six-four," he corrected. He revealed a hiding spot for pistols in the backseat; the car a regular James Bondmobile. "In case one-times pull you over and you gotta hide shit."

After pressing a button on the dashboard, the trunk door flung open. "Gangster pop trunk . . . in case you gotta get guns quick."

Plopping into the driver's seat, he stomped on the gas pedal, revving the engine and filling the air with demonic noise. "Not everybody can ride in these. You get a punk in this car on the boulevard? They'll get jacked in an hour."

Alison sat in the rented car reading a magazine. Scratching a pock-marked cheek, Block ended a chat on a cellular. "That was the Boo-Yaa. They'll be here in ten minutes. They got off on the wrong exit on the freeway. They might be a little mad at *The Source*, dude."

As Frost walked towards the gate, Alison rolled down the window. "He shouldn't fire guns in front of his kid," she said anxiously. "It just continues the circle."

IV

"Where's the guy from *The Source*?" the Samoan giants yelled, marching up the driveway in military formation. The largest member, Folsa, almost seven feet tall, approached with clenched fists. *The Source* had dissed their song "213" on the soundtrack for *White Men Can't Jump* and these hulks were here to settle the score. I rushed to mention that I hadn't written the review.

"Fuck *The Source*," the braided giant yelled, the others laughing and egging him on. "Tell 'em Boo-Yaa's coming out hard! Tell whoever wrote that review that we're gonna find him!"

I told Frost I'd leave. "Naw, don't go," he replied. "It'll be cool. Don't worry."

The itinerary for the day was set; provisions against gun-blasting cholos planned out. "There's thirty thousand cholos there," Frost warned. "But we're gonna go strapped, dude. Those fools are gonna bomb today but we're gonna be rolling with Boo-Yaa. I figure I'll carry a gun or Block since you're gonna be with us, in case shit happens."

As Frost huddled with the Boo-Yaa, strategizing, Block relayed a horrible anecdote about two friends: "They came out of the restaurant and these fools came up and asked, 'Where you from?' They said, 'We just chillin', eating food.' The fools said, 'Fuck that,' went back to their car, got gats and came back. . . . Eighteen bullets each." I began to feel this would be my last day on earth.

On the freeway, "Is there gonna be something?" Alison asked. Glaring at her, "Maybe," Block responded. "What's the matter? You don't like western movies?"

In the backseat, Frost said more about the car show, an annual outdoor fair with cars on exhibit. "It's in Pomona. . . . It's a city of gangsters. . . . The 25-7 Sport G Crips, the Eyelids (all Bloods), Cherryville, Northside 12th Street . . . All at each other's throats! Every day, there's a gang-related murder out there. Today's car show is for *Low Rider*: six hundred thousand subscribers. Every gang in L.A. will be there; Arizona, Mexico, Oakland, Bakersfield, San Jose, Frisco, Stockton . . ."

Usually a performer, Frost said he was intent on casting a visible presence, promoting the new album, mingling with fans and signing autographs. "They say I start a riot when I'm billed at a show," he beamed, "so they're saving me for the big show in October." A carload of *jeinillas* rolled by; one of them, vying for Frost's attention, stuck her head out of her window, started screaming and whipped out her Kodak camera.

He turned, waved, said, "Fuck it," then turned grim. "I hope that after the King verdict they don't turn the car show into a riot. I hope they all come together to have fun and not fuck it up."

Closer to Pomona, freeway traffic grew congested; the air filled with smog. A dozen car radios tuned to different stations were heard: rock, pop-rap, *ranchera*, announcer's voices and commercials for the car show. A Mexican O.G. in tank top, hairnet and locs, cruised by in a large black-and-silver hearselike ride; like a funereal Studebaker with sharp silver jaws on its grill . . . "That's a 'bomb' right there," Frost said, introducing the term into hip-hop vernacular (via the hip-hop media). Traffic jammed bumper to bumper. Up ahead, a group of cholos left their pickup truck and began tagging on a wall. "You know it's gonna be on if it's already starting on the freeway," Frost said, puffing on a pipe.

Watching white girls roll by in sports cars, Block said, "These girls ain't going to see cars, they comin' to scam!" A carload of cholos recognized Frost. This time he quickly nodded, acknowledging with a quick "W'sup" as the cholos flashed hand signs in return.

Gangsta: Merchandising the Rhymes of Violence

With Brenton Wood's cheesy oldies on the car radio, Frost and Block pulled out a large plastic sack of yesca, a brownish green strain of marijuana, which they quickly ignited and smoked. In seconds Frost was flashing handsigns and scowling at cars in other lanes.

▼

On the car-show grounds: sexy Mexican girls with thick legs, hefty breasts and adorable babydoll hairdos; low-rider enthusiasts; members of two hundred gangs; older Mexican men with their wives; young women with children; Black gangsters; industry types; beer and T-shirt salesmen; randomly parked low-riders that were for sale. As we walked towards the stage, I noticed that we were surrounded by cholos. They drank cold Budweiser beers, chomped on hot tacos, laughed loudly; held their women tight, and squinted at anyone who returned a stare.

Many were from East L.A., where the socioeconomic situation, a draconian police force, and long-standing barrio rivalries made peace impossible. Today, they hoped to put trench warfare aside for a minute, hear good music and create a happy memory.

Up ahead, a multitude of people stood shoulder to shoulder, facing a stage, watching a local group lip-sync over a funk track. Behind them, banners promoted *Low Rider* magazine and local "Hot format" radio stations. Frost leading, we squeezed through a hostile throng stopping only when Frost lavished attention on women in revealing outfits. Smiling and flattering, he jotted down beeper numbers or gave his out. As he chatted with one woman, a stampede of people rushed toward my position on the sidelines. Five feet away, like the Arab spy in *The Man Who Knew Too Much*, a Mexican teen staggered out of an opening in the crowd. The cholos who had been tagging on the freeway swung fists and kicked out at his legs. The kid fell to the ground and was repeatedly stabbed. I watched him bleed; wanted to help, but these kids were crazy as hell. A cop on horseback rode in, sending the crowd scurrying to avoid being trampled, but the officer was too late. The cholos had scattered—running by smiling—blending in with the crowd.

Frost reappeared at my side. "You alright?" he asked. Nervous as hell, I said yes. "Thirty thousand," he quipped, shaking his head, referring to the number of 'bangers expected at today's event. "Power 106 — they play techno out here — they gave away a lot of free tickets."

Minutes later, Frost's proteges, the Hispanic MCs, were performing, giving shout-outs and trying to gain the crowd's confidence with poor Mejicano, anti-jura posturing. After inhaling more smoke, Frost suddenly decided he did want to be onstage today; and since he was producing the group, *then fuck it, they won't mind if I just walk out onstage, out of nowhere, and lend my homies some support.* And this is what he did: stumbling behind the group to thunderous applause, grabbing a mic and saying, "This is a public service announcement. . . . My album's in stores now! . . . Ain't no sunshine," he quipped, dropping the title of his latest slow-paced single. Then he floated off, leaving the upstaged group to conclude their own "Ain't No Sunshine"-like dirge.

Near the stage, in a patch of shade, the imposing Boo-Yaas practiced soul-stirring doo-wop harmonies. Roger Troutman, performer of the ubiquitous "More Bounce to the Ounce" (sampled on half of the records streaming from L.A.) exited a makeshift dressing room, walked over and joined in. Capitalizing on the audience's fascination with the Prince formula (Black Hendrixian guitarists), Troutman wore a white leather outfit (with fringes) and what looked like eyeliner (to match his greased hair). Toting a white guitar, the aging funkster mounted a stage and played a somnolent funk ballad. Again, the crowd swayed to avoid stray fists, knives or sticks.

VI

Seeing this, Frost ran to the stage and again grabbed the mic. In the distance, I could see the violence. An occasional stick or bottle rose above this tumultuous sea of people. A white police officer in riot gear yelled through a bullhorn: "I know there's a lot of stress . . ."

The crowd scattered this way and that, the sun blinded my eyes. I'll never forget that only one voice could be heard: Frost urging the crowd to calm themselves, reminding them that they're supposed to stand united as Chicano people. "Raza! We need to show *la jura* that they're full of shit!" Minutes later, the crowd calmed. Inhaling deeply, Roger Troutman gripped his guitar, ran back onto the stage, played the opening strains to "More Bounce," and backed away as more fights erupted.

By now I didn't care that the stampede was heading directly for us. As hysterical people strained at the sawhorses separating artists from the crowd, the Boo-Yaa linked hands and formed their "line," an impenetrable human wall. The skies were sunny and people were getting stabbed. "After the fight ends, all you see are bodies," said Gangsta Rid, one of the giants, as we waited for Frost to rejoin us. "Different gangs . . . then the cops come in to do a body count." The wail of sirens filled the air. A fleet of police cars arrived to end the show. Police officers in riot gear, vests and helmets marched through the crowd, telling people to leave the area, the show was over . . . herding them toward the exit. As we moved through the crowd, heading for the parking lot, the Boo-Yaa led the way. Sticking close together, they watched our backs. When Frost paused to chat with a curvaceous groupie, and the Boo-Yaa tried to find a few for themselves, I turned around and saw a gang of sixty people marching and "bombing" on anything in their path. Innocent bystanders were pushed and punched, yanked by the hair, and knocked over garbage cans. "Oh shit," one of the Boo-Yaa said when he saw them. "If only we had two more Boo-Yaas, we could take them," he sighed, watching and listening as the rowdy set yelled out their name, knocking over trashcans and picnic tables. Everyone around us quickened their step. A woman lifted her baby carriage and started running. A man next to her stood there, apparently admiring a yellow low-rider. He didn't see the mob approach until it was too late. Later that night, the news reported that he had been killed. The woman with the baby carriage appeared onscreen; her face was distraught. "He was just standing right there when they came up to him for no reason and started stabbing him," she sobbed.

We had leaped into a tent where a group of older Mexican men — selling rice, beans, chicken and Budweiser — had set up shop: The Boo-Yaa reached into trashcans filled with ice and snatched cans of beer. Frost dipped into the trays filled with food. Snatching up a beer, I cracked it and told one old man, "Sorry, but fuck that! I'm nervous. . . ." As we drank, we looked through the tent door and saw the rowdy gang march past, noisy as shit, knocking things over and causing everyone to flee in terror. In the parking lot, they killed another man. A witness crouching low in the front seat of his car pulled out a camera and filmed it. His footage — aired on the news — showed a

Riding Shotgun

thin, shirtless Mexican youth squinting his eyes, raising a gun and repeatedly squeezing the trigger. His buddy, also shirtless, with sagging khakis and a beer gut, puffed on a joint and cackled maniacally.

We headed for the car. Frost kept stopping to sign autographs. A line of thirteen police cars sped by, one after another; across the parking lot, riot officers swung nightsticks and Plexiglas shields, as if fighting dragons, trying to contain a growing mob. The skies turned blood-red as the California sun began to set. "Out here, it's not just about making the records," one of the Boo-Yaa said, staring at the chaos and the crowds eventually heading home: "It's about staying alive after they're released."

Chapter 2

No Apologies, No Remorse

■

"Many Angelenos in the ravaged areas are expected to oppose permits for so-called nuisance businesses: liquor stores, pawn shops, auto repair shops and cheap motels. Says one gang member: 'We were doing some renovation to the neighborhood. There are too many liquor stores in our community.'"

—Time *(May 25, 1992)*

Two weeks after attending the Fiesta Car Show in Pomona with Kid Frost, where I saw a man stabbed five feet away from me, I was back in Los Angeles, gathering information for *Spin* magazine. I was in my hotel room reading statistics in the *L.A. Times* and found myself wondering if David Mamet was right. He had written that "We Americans know the real news never reaches the newspapers." I turned the page of the newspaper and saw the words: "Last year, at least 8,600 people were hit by bullets—almost one an hour—while thousands of others were nearly shot [in Los Angeles]."

On another page I read about how the LAPD were "taking seriously intelligence reports that gangs with large arsenals plan to wage war on officers after National Guard troops leave the city." In addition to furniture, food and clothing, looters had stolen thousands of guns.

Another story reported on how the Crips and Bloods had united for a picnic, basketball game and meeting in a Compton neighborhood. The LAPD arrived—there had been complaints about the noise, they claimed—and asked the gangs to leave. They ventured into another area, to continue drinking, listening to music and drag-racing, and were followed by 150 riot police and the National Guard, though one neighborhood resident told the *Times* (May 18, 1992), "They didn't hurt anyone, they were just dancing and drinking with radios playing." The police officers had envisioned an all-out confrontation, but the gang members offered no resistance. They left the area so quickly that officers were frustrated; they hadn't even had time to issue their "Disperse" order.

The newspaper account reported these details on the front page of the Metro section, but tacked on an ending about two nude white men found beaten and unconscious blocks away from the gathering. The two white men were beaten "and robbed," the article emphasized, "according to witnesses." This was consistent with the *Times'* approach to covering the truce: they covered the picnics, gatherings and parties between the sets but ended the stories with news of any shooting, whether it was gang-related or not.

I smoked a cigarette and stared out at the Comedy Store next door, disturbed by what I'd read. The presence of National Guardsmen had restored calm to South Central's troubled streets, but the LAPD's "Surveillance Unit" still told the *Times* that Bloods and Crips planned to "wage war on the LAPD" once the soldiers left town.

I called the LAPD and was referred to a public-relations department and they, in turn, steered me towards Detective Paul Glascow. I called him up and he sounded somewhat embarrassed about the alarmist statement. How could it could be leaked to the media? I asked. And what "reports" were the LAPD "taking seriously"? "I can't say anything," he said. "There were a lot of speculations, stories being told, reports on things being said about stations going to be attacked, but nothing happened."

The LAPD "just tried to stay prepared, what with the Samoan trial and the arraignment of the Denny suspects, but we haven't got any additional vests or ammunition or anything." He had a cavalier attitude about the situation; he spoke as if the storm had passed. The LAPD had it all under control again. In addition to "CRASH [Community Resources Against Street Hoodlums] and gang units trying to maintain expertise, monitoring who might be gang members, or through the use of informants," they were also "working with the ATF [Alcohol, Tobacco and Firearms], with the Treasury or the FBI to locate and recover weapons and, with the riots, to locate criminal offenders."

"If there is in fact a truce," he said, unconvinced, "we hope it leads to gang members curtailing their violence, which leads to victimizing members of their own community." His answer was by the book, devoid of emotion or actual concern, and I found myself wanting to hang up on this cop. "We hope they can concentrate on more positive activities instead of violence or narcotics, which major emphasis is placed on," he continued. "As a police officer or detective, that's what I'd say."

His answers were very general, even curt; he said only what he had to. Race relations among Los Angeles gangs were strained, but Glascow was slow to admit this. "I won't say we've had any increase in fights between them," he began, as ambiguously as a Kafka character, "but there were many 'speculations' about Latin gangs who were approached and would not agree to a truce of some sort." I hung up the phone, cracked open a 40 and sat near the window. It had been a hard day; I couldn't believe I was back in Los Angeles again. Randi, my girl at the time, was always flying out here for her friends' weddings, and she always returned with stories about going to beaches, amusement parks, exotic restaurants and art galleries. All I could tell her about were ghettos. Someday, I'll be able to visit Los Angeles and see the side that white people see.

I had arrived that afternoon, and didn't even have time to finish a cigarette before Ramona, a publicist for Quality Records, yelled, "Hey Ronin!" from her gray car parked at the curb. I had met Ramona two weeks ago, when Mellow Man Ace took me to the label's offices to meet his friends in A Lighter Shade of Brown. She had sparkling eyes, beautiful dark skin and nice full lips. She was in her early twenties and accessorized her polyester business suit with subtle jewelry and light makeup. She was the kind of woman I'd talk to in a bar. I had to remind myself that being overfriendly was part of her job description.

She drove me to the Sunset Hyatt, commanded a valet to park her car, and entered the hotel lobby, a beige chamber with plush rugs, lousy pastel paintings and cracked marble pillars. She proudly walked past the white guests blocking her path to the registration desk. She had two personas: with me she was relaxed and readily confessed to a childhood among the disenfranchised; to the white Rock Hudson clone behind the desk she emphasized her professional demeanor, characterized by a tone that implied that here was someone accustomed to being waited on. The blond man in the royal blue suit verified her reservation in a nearby computer, returned and began to inform her that yes, her room was ready, but that if she wanted, she could change her reservations and book one of the hotel's more inexpensive rooms. She said no, the room she had was just fine. He said okay and stared over her head, fixing the Mexican bellhops with a hard stare. "Now we'll just have to see your credit card again," he told Ramona, "just to make sure everything's in order, you understand." She sighed, opened her purse and searched for it, accustomed to being mistrusted.

"Hey, dude, I need a room for a singer I'm managing," yelled a loud obnoxious voice behind us. A white rock 'n' roll longhair tilted his black cowboy hat at the registrar. "Here's the card I'll be using." He slapped a Gold Card onto the counter and walked away, as disrespectful to the registrar as the registrar had been to Ramona. Silently, the registrar took the card, asked Ramona to wait, then worked on the latest request. Halfway across the room, longhair turned and yelled, as if suddenly remembering that the clerk existed. "I'll be over here if you need some handwriting!"

I was lighting another cigarette when longhair wandered up and asked if I was from New York. I said yes and slipped my lighter back into my jacket pocket. "Yeah, I'm from New York too, from Milestone Productions on the Lower East Side. Ever hear of us?"

"Not really."

Across the room, Ramona's confidence began to slip; she dressed, spoke and paid like a professional but the registrar kept her waiting. By now, longhair's songwriter, who resembled an Anthrax reject, stood by the desk, spoke over Ramona, and demanded the penthouse. The reject had just received a record contract. "Hey dude," he asked the beleaguered clerk, "you wanna go for a ride in my Corvette?"

The miserable afternoon continued. I sat in Ramona's car with the window open. Patches of sweat drenched the armpits of my shirt. She

Gangsta: Merchandising the Rhymes of Violence

was taking me to a photo shoot for A Lighter Shade of Brown, she explained, navigating the car through Beverly Hills traffic and searching for R&B music on the radio. Burned out from another 40-filled send-off in New York the night before, I nodded obediently, knowing that her label expected a lot for the price of the hotel room. "They're in a parking lot on Wilshire and Sixth." I pretended to know the area. "And later on you'll meet the South Central Cartel. The S.C.C.'s gonna take you to the Black part of town."

"It's hot out here," she said, facing the road.

I nodded, staring at the monied pedestrians in faded jeans and sunglasses, and half listened to her confession that she had been worried this morning. Before heading to the airport to greet me, she'd heard a news report about another pipe bomb found on the freeway, the third in the last week, placed on different roadways. "The police had to blow this one up."

A huge billboard promoted Rick Dees' morning radio show. I thought this has-been had died already, but there he was, more energetic than ever, staring down at traffic like *Gatsby*'s T.J. Eckleberg.

"Unless there's a breeze soon, I just wanna tell you this is earthquake weather," she said, turning into the more upscale Third and Hancock region, "just so you know if the ground starts moving."

We were south of Hollywood, on spotless streets in well-secured suburbs. "It's the rich part over here. Lou Rawls, a lot of the older stars and lawyers live here."

Without warning, the suburban sights were replaced by liquor stores, cracked sidewalks and graffiti-covered walls. We were near Western, the "more Hispanic and Korean" area. There were burnt buildings, debris-filled Dumpsters and Mexican laborers hammering nails into rooftops. "This is more Hispanic," she repeated, "closer to downtown."

Mexican girls with large earrings sat on bus-stop benches, an ice-cream truck sold tacos, packs of Mexican men drank from bottles. We passed a street named Beaudry and it was all gone, as if someone had taken a giant eraser to it.

We were now in a business district. Business towers gleamed, yuppies crowded the sidewalks and streets and white RTD buses honked their horns and blocked traffic. She stopped the car for a red light and yuppies of all races and creeds rushed by. As we passed the imposing

No Apologies, No Remorse

Sheraton Grande hotel, she almost hit a pimply-faced white bicycle messenger. He was distracted by the jabbering voice on his walkie-talkie. Leo Castelli stared at us from a Gap ad on a bus stop. "This is where I left them," she said of the group, spinning into the 2nd Street tunnel. On the sidewalk, a white man in a raggedy white suit lugged a huge heavy wooden cross on his back. "Repent for your sins!" he yelled, hoping yuppies would read the biblical quotes painted on his cross. "Repent for your sins!" he repeated, the cross scraping the sidewalk behind him as he walked.

"People are more cautious down here," Ramona explained. "They were very hard-hit with looting and robbery. There's an 'uneasy' feeling. People are just waiting to see what happens next. It's not over. Everyone knows it: the people, the media, the politicians. They're trying to put all the people into 'Koreatown' or 'Little Mexico' or whatever, but there's not just Koreans in Koreatown, there's Hispanics." She drove me to Roscoe's, a restaurant in South Central known for its chicken-and-waffles, and introduced me to the South Central Cartel, a local group heavily influenced by NWA. "We're still from here, unlike a lot of groups who get onstage and claim South Central but be comin' from the Valley," one member said with a Mississippi accent. They wore black windbreakers, wool caps, sunglasses and khakis, and like many other gangsta rappers, cursed a lot to show they were world-weary and trigger-happy.

They'd later sign with Def Jam West and wear personalized starter jackets in *The Source*'s Coast To Coast photo section, but for their first major feature, they led me to a white limousine they had rented for our tour through the ghetto.

The limo rolled through South Central and group members jabbered words faster than my pen could write; they smoked weed and laughed at the sight of decimated Asian stores. They agreed that Ice Cube's "Black Korea" song was realistic but claimed that they didn't condone the burning or looting of Asian businesses. They'd even filmed a Public Service Announcement, they announced, that stressed the importance of unity. But still, some Korean grocers had "disrespected" Black customers. Grocers were instantly suspicious of Blacks, and they were rude: "They snatched money out of people's hands" and "never said 'Thank you' or 'You're welcome.' "

And of course, a Korean grocer had killed fifteen-year-old Latasha

Gangsta: Merchandising the Rhymes of Violence

Harlins. The woman could have been sentenced to sixteen years but walked with five years' probation, a $500 fine, ten weeks' work at a social center, and monthly visits to her parole officer.

"People were more mad about that than Rodney King," Havoc confirmed. He stepped out of the limo and approached the damaged facade of the Empire Liquor Store, the site of the murder.

"Everybody around here knew her," said Rhyme Son. He pointed through a rusty iron gate at the trash, debris and the counter where it took place. Harlins swung a hand towards the grocer then turned to leave. The grocer pulled a nearby pistol and shot once. "They burnt the shit down," said Rhyme. The group posed in front of the store; they smiled and waited for me to snap a picture. I refused to. The limo pulled away. In the rearview mirror, you could read the words Meat Shop painted on the store.

■■

"So pay respect to the Black Fist or we'll burn your store right down to a crisp."
                                        —*Ice Cube, "Black Korea"*

The limo stopped at Florence and Normandy, where trucker Reginald Denny was yanked from his truck, knocked to the ground, surrounded and bashed on the skull with an oxygenator. Nearby stores were burnt skeletons of their former glory, save for a liquor store favored by neighborhood residents. On its wall, someone had spray-painted the title of an NWA song, "Fuck Tha Police."

"He was driving through here saying some shit about 'The Police won!'" one South Central cartel member claimed. "How the fuck you gonna drive through here saying that? They didn't like that so they snatched him out. All you see is what's on the video. You don't see what happened before that." The words were similar to some that the jury heard in the Simi Valley courtroom.

Trak Auto no longer existed, and a pile of rubble on the corner of 81st and Vermont "used to be the hamburger stand." We passed nine other burnt businesses and the group was silent until Rhyme noticed a specific lot and said, "The Korean store— Gone!"

Now that the news cameras were nowhere around, Edward James Olmos wasn't supervising a clean-up squad at a certain ruin. "Police got scared during the riots," Prodeje said. "I saw them going into stores and I laughed. Fucking police come in and hit us on our heads; now they're scared like bitches!" Another gas station had been destroyed. "They got the liquor stores too! They had a field day!" Some ruins had the words Black Owned painted on them.

One battered Korean-owned grocery brought back memories for the group. It was there that a Black employee murdered two other Black men. The employee was protecting his employers, the group explained, laughing derisively. One of the men died on the premises, the other died later and the shooter was arrested. "He was stupid," said Prodeje. "These fucking cops just saw two less Black motherfuckers they got to deal with."

The thought of manipulative Koreans led to the group telling of how Koreans stopped young Blacks on the street after the riot and offered free hot dogs and sodas. "They were telling us, 'We want peace; tell your friends, tell your family,' but I didn't want to hear that shit," said Rhyme. "I told them, 'You should have thought about that long ago.'"

When they saw that a store called Sound Expo burned, they filled the limo with hollow laughter. "No sounds coming out of that no more!" I shook my head in disapproval, just as Prodeje chanted, "Ashes to ashes and dust to dust, when they build that shit back? It's gonna be . . . re-spect for us!"

The limo pulled to a stop in a residential neighborhood. Outside of the one- or two-story tract homes, you could see teens in blue and red gang-related rags, hats and T-shirts. "Hey, w'sup," Havoc yelled to his friends near a Jeep with smoke-tinted windows. The back door opened again, sunlight creeped in and a young Crip named Nite Owl 3 stuck his head inside the car.

The neighborhood was filled with gang members and I was scared to get out. The television news linked some of the men who attacked Denny with the gang and, though I'm Puerto Rican, I've been told my skin is somewhat pale. I'd seen Crips and Bloods posing in photos with rags tied around their faces; I'd heard the stories of how Crips killed anyone wearing red. The South Central Cartel asked me to step out of the car; they wanted their friends to see that a reporter from a music magazine was expressing interest in them—so reluctantly, and with my eyes facing the floor, so as not to challenge anyone, I did. My poker face seemed to be working and no one noticed that I was nervous. The purpose of my trip was to write an account of the gangs and not a local gangsta rap group so I called Nite Owl over and asked if I could interview him.

He spoke generally about the gangs until a stereotype entered the conversation. There were many stereotypes, he said. One was that the entire gang would jump anyone who wants to join. That was from the movie *Colors*. For him, getting in was as simple as being fifteen, and agreeing to fight another kid so that the older members could watch. "They kind'a tricked me into it and I didn't give a fuck, I used to fight every day anyway!"

He stood on the curb and, noticing that a teen Blood was eavesdropping, quickly leaped into mournful war stories. "About ten people from the 8-7s got killed," said Nite, using both hands to adjust a baseball cap over the identifying blue bandanna on his head. "I seen so much. One of my homeboys was buying weed. He went into another 'hood. They were enemies and somebody asked him what city he was from, and he told 'em. When he was getting back into his truck, they started shooting."

Other kids gangbanged because they needed protection, or because it was just in their blood, but he started because he wanted the flashy possessions many 'bangers owned. "Money rolls, fresh cars, I wanted all that stuff." If he wanted to leave, all he had to do was stop associating with Crips. "But if you have enemies and tell them you ain't banging no more, they might not wanna listen."

He said that the media was distorting their image, that gangbangers were "regular people." If a gangbanger could help you, he would. They wouldn't hurt someone without just cause, and the gangs weren't about dominating their turf. "We're just a group of brothers kicking it every day like a family. We ain't no 'dirty people.' We're human beings too! If I see a Blood, I ain't just gonna run up on him cause he's wearing red!" He glanced over at the teenage Blood at the curb for emphasis. "And I ain't never been racist! Even before the riots. Where I'm from, the 8-7 Gangsters, the 8-Trey Gangsters, we would be cool with people. But then I'd meet a girl. Come to find out her man is in another gang. That leads to beef over a female. It's not really about the 'hoods. It's about what's happening in them."

The fact that there was a truce meant that the teenage Blood could stand in this neighborhood without being attacked. On that afternoon, the Blood was just another neighborhood resident, not an enemy, and Nite Owl 3 seemed relieved. He heard about the truce two days after Rodney King was pulled over on the road, beaten, and tasered; the Crips and Bloods united and threw a party. "I never thought it could happen. Everything's cool so far." Again, he used the nearby Blood as an example. "If I trip on a Blood, my boys'll check me and his boys'll check him." He ran off a list of names of gangs involved in the truce — the 8-7 Street Gang, East Coast Crips, Neighborhood Crips, Hoovers, Raymond Crips, 9-7 Gangsters, 11-Deuce Broadway Gangster Crew, 4-Trey Gangsters, 4-Deuce Gangsters, Avalon Gangster Crew, the Bounty Hunters ("They're Bloods"), Pueblo Bishops and Denver Lanes — and said he hoped the cease-fire could last. The only real problem, he claimed, was that the police were trying to turn the groups against each other. "If the gangs come together the police know they're gonna come shoot their ass!"

He frowned and said he had heard about the LAPD's claims that Crips and Bloods planned to "wage war" against the police once the soldiers left town. "That's some shit," he suppressed a laugh. "We not trying to 'take over'! We just trying to get our thing together. Now people look at us differently. They don't see us killing each other no more. Every time police stop me on the street and jack me up, they ask the same thing. That's not true. I ain't never heard anything about that. I think the cops are starting it. I don't think they want the peace to happen. They *wanna* see us killing each other."

In November 1987, Los Angeles District Attorney Ira Reiner said, "We are the gang capital of the United States in terms of numbers, in terms of violence, in terms of overall impact on the entire criminal justice system." If the LAPD's *Citywide Gang Crime Summary* for May 7, 1992, is to be believed, Reiner's claim is still valid. The Summary reported that 56,264 Los Angelenos were gang members; 32,061 Hispanics made up 200 gangs; 15,742 Crips were in 108 gangs; 5,213

Bloods were in 44 gangs; 2,185 Asians were in 34 gangs; 777 "Stoners" were in 19 gangs; and 286 whites were in four gangs.

I sat in the hotel bar with a cigarette, debating on whether to start drinking now or wait for Manuel Velasquez—a gang counselor from Community Youth Gang Services that Kid Frost suggested I speak with. Just as I was rising from the table to purchase a beer with *Spin*'s expense money, I saw a short, stocky man enter the room, stand in the doorway and comb the tables with his eyes. He resembled the actor who played the gang leader on *Hill Street Blues*, I noted, as he shook my hand, sat down and provided a little background information: he was in his thirties, a counselor for over a decade now and happily married. I sat at the table drinking beer after beer as he sipped the first of many sodas.

He had an unorthodox approach to settling gang rivalries; instead of shaking hands, he encouraged 'bangers to fight, but with the hands. "That way, one will get fucked up, one will win, and both walk away."

He told me that gang history in Los Angeles reached back to the early 1900s and that the stereotypes surrounding them are the biggest problem. The local newspapers and television shows were ecstatic that the Bloods and the Crips were forming a truce, but were only reporting on it because the gangs' colorful rags were an easily digestible visual hook—especially when different-colored rags were tied together to signify unity. And when viewers saw the rags pressed together, they—and the station's newswriters—naturally assumed that all gang violence would cease.

But the Crips and Bloods were only a small part of the gang culture. "When we talk about gang history, Latino gangs have been around since the late thirties and early forties," Velasquez stressed. "The gangs that I deal with are third and fourth generation: great-grandfather, grandfather, father and son were all members of one particular gang. When we talk about gangs, we're talking about gangs that have been around for sixty to eighty years. They're well-rooted families and look just like you and me—it's just that they're in this shit."

Velasquez noticed that many people disagreed with his views on gangs; his opinions were unpopular because they contradicted the stereotypes in newspapers, commercials, movies like *Colors* and *Boyz N the Hood* and anything else that could exploit the culture. It upset him when shrewd marketers romanticized the violence. Today's kids were vulnerable and easily influenced. "I laugh at these movies because they take everything out of context," he said, "the names they use, the way they dress them; then they tell you it's based on some actual shit." When kids who didn't know any better began to emulate the on-screen action, "that's what I have to deal with." The kids would dress like gangbangers, associate with them and not even realize that they'd crossed the line.

There were certain things he wanted me to know, he said. The Bloods and the Crips were always in the media but so-called "Hispanics"—he bristled at the misnomer—actually had the largest number of sets. Some Mexican gangs were even upset at how the media was ignoring their own truce. "Latinos" comprised 65 to 70 percent of the population in Los Angeles, "but all you see in the *Times* and everything else is 'Black! Black! Black!'"

The media also never really discussed the white gangs, which definitely existed. Velasquez sighed and told of the white-boy cholos infiltrating high schools in the Valley. During a lecture, one white kid forgot that Velasquez was once a gangbanger and was disrespectful. "And I told him: 'Hey homeboy, I don't wanna disrespect you or anything but you're fucking white! My job as a counselor is to tell you, 'Get out of those Dickies and those Nike shoes; get back into your "Opie" pants, pick up your skateboard and hang out where you're supposed to hang out.'"

Leon Bing pointed out that gang nicknames and slang were popular with white kids, and that they'd begun to form "small wannabe groups with names like South Side Gang and Palmetto Boyz." Like the Crips and Bloods, they used hand signals and affected the fashion. Other whites formed skinhead gangs with names like the Orange County Skinheads, the Crazy Fuckin Skins, the Suicidals (aka The Boys), FSU (Fuck Shit Up) and the Huntington Beach Hardcores. But the stereotypes of Black, hip-hop-listening gangsters made for better newspaper reading, which may explain why you never heard about East L.A.'s Stoner problem, Velasquez added, "having to do with heavy-metal music and hard rock. In the Valley, I had a gang called the Lurch Street Rockers, satanic motherfuckers going around, tagging up '666,' going into neighborhoods, kicking back and lighting up altars."

The history of gang activity had gone from hobby to field of ex-

Gangsta: Merchandising the Rhymes of Violence

pertise; he narrated with the unshakable confidence of a social historian who believed that only through studying the past could one predict the future. The 1940s were an era when men took pride in "duking it out" with their hands, he pointed out, as if he had been present. An opponent hit the ground and the victor showed off for spectators by taunting him. "You want some more?! Get up! I'll let you!" The code of honor may have been primitive but it was upheld; and handguns weren't viewed as arbiters of social conflict. Until the 1970s, knives were acceptable ("to cut him up a little but not to kill him; just to let him know"); knives, chains and crowbars. Occasionally someone died from their injuries, but murder wasn't as commonplace.

"Everybody partied together," he recalled. "You were able to go from one neighborhood to another." If a problem arose, you said, "Fuck it, right now," and fought with the hands. When the fight ended, you could wind up drinking from the same bottle with your opponent. Until the 1960s, Black and Mexican kids coexisted, but with the formation of the Crips and later, the reactionary Bloods, Blacks strayed from Mexican styles and worked to develop distinct forms of expression. Narcotic sales were introduced to a new generation of gangbangers; the situation took a nosedive and the body count began to escalate. Guns became more available and crack was introduced. "In '84, shit hit the fan with the Bloods and Crips," Velazquez frowned. "We had the Olympics here and Chief Daryl Gates locked up everybody that was a 'known gangster' for two weeks. Coke became cheap and it wasn't just a white, rich thing anymore. Everybody on each block wanted to sell the shit. When you have too many of one product on one block, the guy with the biggest gun is gonna end up selling it. Because of that, gang-related homicides shot up. Before then? There was none of that."

Velasquez pinpointed 1985 as the turning point. In 1980, 351 people were killed. In 1981, it decreased to 291. Nineteen eighty-two had fewer homicides, only 205; and 1983 had 216. Nineteen eighty-four, when crack was introduced, had 212. In 1985, however, once people started opening their spots and competing for sales, 271 people were killed. In 1986, the figure rose to 328. In 1987 and 1988, the number was 387. Nineteen eighty-nine would have 452 deaths, and the new decade would enter with a whopping 690 murders, more than twice the number of a decade ago. In 1991, you had something close to 760 gang-related deaths. And today? "We average 50 homicides a month in Los Angeles: 4.5 gang incidents a day, and one of those is a drive-by.

"Out here," he said contemptuously, "there's something white people have called N.I.M.B.Y. — Not In My Back Yard. When shit hit the fan in South Central, they didn't care until looters started coming down into Hollywood and Beverly Hills. Then you saw who got protection and who didn't." I would've thought this statement to be self-serving demagoguery if I hadn't heard a commercial on the radio. I was searching for some hip-hop, to see what music the region was treated to, and heard a loud rock-themed commercial proclaim, "Power 106, Budweiser and the Mayor's Office urge listeners to volunteer and help rebuild the city! This Saturday, June 6, Hollywood gets a fresh coat of paint!"

The police were angry with Velasquez because he wouldn't rat on criminal offenders and the kids suspected him of being a snitch. In his decade as a counselor, he never ratted on anyone; but on a daily basis, he had to prove his trustworthiness to the kids he worked with. He'd walk in with his shirt lifted up, to show that there was no wire on him, and the kids would sigh with relief then infer that a policeman had claimed that Manuel was their informer. The police would try to divide him from those he tried to help. But he would turn the tables and tell the kids, "If you're gonna believe a white man, a man with a badge, maybe he's the snitch and you gotta look into that!"

He couldn't understand why the police would try to sabotage his efforts; and their machinations meant that Manuel had to be careful. He wouldn't tell kids, "Don't join a gang," because he'd sound moralistic. He would apply psychology, and compliment them on having the guts to get jumped in; then he'd say he hoped they had the guts to face the consequences they'd face when they wanted to leave, when "the asswhipping is a thousand times worse and longer."

"I'll be there but I won't jump in," he'd promise aspirants. "I'll just make sure they don't get crazy on your ass. And if I see an eyeball pop out? I'll jump in and say, 'Ya estuvo! You hurt him enough!'"

He was happy that his scared-straight approach deterred many from joining. "When I say that thing about the eyeball, they start telling me, 'Oh no, I don't wanna get jumped!'" he chuckled. "And

Gangsta: Merchandising the Rhymes of Violence

I say, 'You should'a thought about that before you started thinking about joining!' "

Gang affiliations were flimsy, and they were dissolved once someone went to prison, he'd mention. If you're Mexican, you join the Mexican Mafia. If you're Black, you join Black Guerrilla Family. If you're white, you join the Aryan Brotherhood. If you're Asian, you join Asians' World.

"And you don't talk to a 'nigger' or a 'white boy' unless it's business." Manuel would try to explain that cholos raped weaker cholos in jail, and Bloods raped other Bloods, but the youth would say, "Fuck you, that doesn't happen." He would explain that he had homeboys who were "tat-down" when they went in, that they were the hardest motherfuckers, but when they came out and you mentioned rape, they'd be quick to say, "No comment!"

The gang was supposed to be your family, but they really didn't give a damn about you when you weren't around, he explained. One kid learned this after a six-year sentence. Manuel sighed, sipped his soda and remembered the day he received the man's phone call. It was the man's release date and he asked Manuel to pick him up from the prison; Manuel arrived on time and took him to dinner, to welcome him home. At the table, the man asked Manuel to drive him to the neighborhood he was arrested at. Manuel told him, "You didn't learn shit. Why you wanna go back?" The man grew indignant; his eyes filled with fire. "Hey man, I killed somebody for this neighborhood. I am somebody," he answered. Reluctantly, Manuel did as instructed; he dropped the man off.

An hour later, the man called Manuel. "Pick me up!" he yelled. "Pick me up!" Manuel got back into his car and drove to the meeting place, which was far from the neighborhood, he noticed. The man's face was purple and his shirt was ripped. The man explained that he arrived and sought old acquaintances. "I got jumped!" he blurted out.

"Who jumped you?" Manuel asked.

"My own neighborhood."

"Your own neighborhood?!"

"Yeah, man. Some dude that had my nickname jumped me 'cause I had the same name!"

Manuel paused in telling the story; he sipped from his soda then shook his head.

"They didn't even know who he was anymore. And this dude had his town name tattooed all over the place: on his chest, his back, his arms, his neck and all over his forehead. They jumped on his ass cause the youngsters didn't know who he was!"

He explained that gang members I'd interview would say anything, because they knew I was a clueless outsider. Some of the root causes theorized by sociologists were true, he conceded, but most kids joined gangs simply because they wanted instant gratification, which came in the form of money from drug sales. "I don't go for this 'I'm poor or I'm Latino or Black and I'm from the housing project,'" Manuel yelled. "Fuck you! You wanna make it? Work for what you want!" We lived in an era where inept parents spoiled their children: ". . . ironing their pants, making them breakfast, catering to them. And the kids grow up to be like 'Gimme, gimme, gimme.' Tell them: 'Fuck you, work for it.'" These kids were down for their neighborhood, they'd tell him every day at work. But when he asked why, the dialogue turned into "Who's on First."

"Well, I'm down for my neighborhood. I'll snuff anybody out!"

"Well, if you're so proud to kill somebody for your neighborhood, tell me something about it. Who started the shit?" The kid wouldn't know.

"Well, what are you proud of your neighborhood for?"

"Oh, my homeboys."

"Well, what about your homeboys?"

"Oh, they're crazy."

"Why are they crazy?"

" 'Cause they drink 40 ounces and shit."

"What makes them do that?"

"Well, uh, just because."

"So how come you have to kill the other guy?"

" 'Cause they're from the other side."

"Why?"

"Just 'cause they're from the other side."

"Is that the only reason?"

"Yeah."

"Well, how do you know he's from the other side?"

Gangsta: Merchandising the Rhymes of Violence

"Because he looks like he's from the other side."

"And if they ask you where you from and you don't answer?" he asked rhetorically.

"That's when you die."

Some of these zealous new 'bangers, he decided, were the most dangerous. "Sometimes you wonder if they even have a brain!" The kids wanted the respect accorded to older veterans, but without earning their stripes, so, to gain instant notoriety, they would most likely kill retired gangsters. This was why homeboys his age or older were fearful when they shouldn't have to be, he admitted, "just because there's some little motherfucker who has to prove something to be somebody."

He spoke of the many funerals he attended: he had to tell young children why their fathers died senselessly. He had to haggle with local authorities to ensure that ceremonies had adequate security. He had to worry about rival sets throwing drive-bys on mourners. His quixotic veneer slowly eroded and stress appeared on his face.

"I have to tell homeboys, 'Don't pick the body up out of the casket; show some respect; show some courtesy.' I've gone to funerals where homeboys pull out cans of spray paint and start tagging up on the casket. One time, this kid got shot under the eye and his homie starts poking through the guy's face, looking for the hole. I got sick of this shit! Not even death can guarantee an escape from your enemies," he said. "They'll go to the cemetery, and if the person has a nice stone, they'll stab at it. Or if it has bronze letters, they'll scratch them off with a knife, just to let the dead kid's homies know it's not over."

The day before, a Mexican boy had been slain in a drive-by. He was riding a tricycle on the lawn outside of his home when a bullet entered the left side of his neck and emerged from his right cheek. Three children ("ranging in age from five months to three years, killed in separate gang attacks") had also been recently gunned down; and now this, Manuel said, visibly affected.

"Although the apparent truce between some factions of the Bloods and Crips has received much attention since the Los Angeles riots," the *L.A. Times* wrote, "warfare between Latino gangs has continued unabated."

Manuel spoke about how tragic it was as I glanced at other tables. New York rapper Chi Ali and two friends had swaggered into the bar, talking loud and thinking L.A. nothing but Jheri-Kurls and *Breakin'*.

"That little boy that was killed yesterday?" Manuel cynically observed. "His brother goes on TV saying, 'I'm not a gangbanger.' Fuck you. Look at his hair, how he's dressed, all of that." This was what he believed. To him, gangbangers were everywhere.

The mood at our table was grim; saddened, I sipped my beer. "That's a cool way of covering a payback," he continued. "A little boy ain't gonna die in vain. On the news, they give you this sad— They put the little sign up [that says,] 'If you wanna donate money . . .' and it's cool. They need it. But, when they get the payback, the other family's gonna need cash too." I stared at him across the table and knew he'd spend this lifetime trying to change the unchangeable. He was a "real American hero" who'd never be interviewed by Barbara Walters. He was profoundly sad.

Chapter 3

Children of the Damned

"In a mood of frustration, you feel the only effective way to deal with street gangs is with a flame thrower."
— *Los Angeles District Attorney Ira Reiner*

The heavy-metal music made conversation impossible but the fearful partygoers in this backyard in Pico still tried to ask each other questions. I sat in a colorful plastic lawn chair next to members of Street Mentality, a gangsta rap group signed to Loud/RCA, and observed a different side of the Mexican-American community in California. The young career women wore skirts, blouses, heels and subtle jewelry; the men were clean cut, with trimmed moustaches, and instead of the white T-shirt and khakis look favored by immature gangbangers, they wore L.L. Bean shoes, Levi's and tasteful dress shirts.

This was a more upscale gathering — office workers and civil servants on a night off — and on the surface, there was nothing gang-related about the evening.

The partygoers looked happy but apprehensive; they shook hands, patted each other on the back and laughed at their own jokes but, at all times, they also kept one eye on us. Distracted, they tried to discuss their jobs and marriages; at any minute we might suddenly begin to act rowdy; we might want to slow-dance too closely with their women or change the music. We might pull steel and try to rob them or start flashing gang signs while claiming a set.

Underdressed for the occasion, in sneakers, baggy jeans and ill-fitting long-sleeve shirts, we sat in a secluded corner. In our self-imposed exile, we smoked, drank, felt unwanted and disliked.

An older woman emerged from the back door of the house and, with a glittering smile, warmly informed her guests that dinner was served. Bandit, Street Mentality's lead rapper, leaped to his feet and raced for the door. A line of guests waited patiently for their turn; once they reached the stove, they grabbed plates and served themselves from heaping cauldrons of white rice, beans and ground beef. Once the kitchen emptied, we piled our plates to capacity then snuck back into the yard. A second later, we felt guilty: someone was scraping the pots with a spoon. We'd eaten all of the rice.

After wolfing down our plates, we snuck back into the kitchen to finish off the ground beef. After we ate that, we resolved to make due with the free liquor. Reclining on the lawn chair, I stared up at the starry sky and thought about how it was nice to not think about gangs.

But the beer made Slow Pain sentimental; he took the chair next to mine and said he'd been born into a family with gang affiliations. He wanted to be a football player and had actually made his high school team, but family enemies appeared on his campus. "And the only way to get back at my cousins was to get at me."

He stared at the lovely young women floating around the yard and at their more conservative men and his confidence began to sink. These guests would typecast him because of his external appearance. They'd think he was a hoodlum in these baggy clothes, and they wouldn't take him seriously. He sighed and told an anecdote about a woman who'd invited him over to her house. "I thought I was going to get some pussy so I lay in the bed and the fucking closet door starts opening." Six of his family's enemies were inside and their guns were placed at his temple. "Tell your cousin we're gonna get him," they said. He sipped his beer and laughed: it was a good thing the girl's mother—a churchgoing woman—arrived and chased them away. But again: "I was gonna be a message to my cousin for fucking around. 'Hey, tell your cousin this!' BOOM!"

The partygoers eventually discovered that we had eaten all of the food; but I suspected that even if we hadn't, they would've felt we had. They sat across from us in the yard, staring at white rock music videos on a television someone had carried outside, and when one of our

Gangsta: Merchandising the Rhymes of Violence

voices happened to rise, they fixed us with a look of contempt. Returning from inside the home, Bandit took the third lawn chair. Nodding, he lit a joint as Slow spoke about Lil' Priest.

From a family with gang ties, Priest tried to distance himself from the 'bangers who loitered on his porch. In Catholic school, he was a B student who never gave the impression that he thought he was invincible. After a car accident, he stood to receive $180,000. To escape gang violence, he planned to buy a house in a new neighborhood. On his eighteenth birthday, he was happy; the settlement money would soon be awarded. Slow Pain bought him a gift—tickets for a Keith Sweat concert—but Priest declined; he wanted to stay home, "to be safe."

"A car drove by," Slow said with moist eyes. "One shot; they shot only one time, and in the middle of the night; it hit him directly in the heart. On the night of his birthday, all of his dreams were shattered."

Bandit nodded and mentioned that Priest had been his only visitor in the hospital. Bandit had been stabbed and Priest had appeared with magazines and candy.

A fifteen-year-old had murdered Priest with the shotgun his father bought him for Christmas, Slow Pain said; and it was his mother who drove the car during the drive-by.

That was fucked up, I mentioned.

But hold up, Slow Pain answered. He hadn't finished yet.

He had attended a recent car show and spent a pleasant afternoon studying cars, watching rap groups perform and flirting with women. He was content as he began the long drive home. Traffic on the freeway was light and he'd be home on time. "But guess who's coming behind me at sixty-five miles per hour?" he asked, loud enough to elicit a stare from the partygoers. "This same fifteen-year-old! I'm nineteen, he's fifteen; no respect for life!" The youth hung out of a window, blasting at Slow's car—"Blam Blam Blam," Slow illustrated—while Slow kept "on the ground," dodged bullets, and hoped he wouldn't crash into cross-lane traffic.

"I had asked my dad if I could take my little cousin to the car show," he reflected. " 'Everything's gonna be safe,' " he had promised. "My little cousin got shot in the spine."

During another incident, the same teenager's car roared up behind

Slow. The kid's first shot smashed through the back windshield and cracked the front sun visor. "My friend's yelling, 'He's coming! He's coming!'" The kid was showing Slow Pain the gun. "First he shows the gun to let us know he's gonna shoot us, then he's going through red lights, chasing us down Rosary Boulevard. Pow Pow Pow." The kid fired at Slow's head but missed. Slow sprawled across the front seat and made it a difficult target, "'cause he has a good shot: He did shoot my homeboy right in the heart with one shot. And yeah, everybody knows he did it. The cops know he did it," he claimed.

Slow Pain didn't care about root causes or theory; he didn't want to understand why some kids joined gangs; he didn't have the distance from the subject to make lengthy deliberation possible.

We sat in our chairs watching everyone else have a good time; the sad chords in the heavy-metal songs they blasted chiseled the fact that we were all outsiders from deep within our adamant hearts.

The group hailed from Pico, where eighteen people had been murdered during a two-week period. The local authorities were apathetic, so the FBI had to conduct an investigation of their own. Pico was a tiny suburb where residents modeled smaller sets after the supergangs in the city. Youth joined these gangs for a number of reasons, they explained. Most kids wanted protection. Some had no choice: they lived near the gangs, so being jumped in was inevitable. Someone could leave the gang by moving away or trying to dissociate from them. "But if you try to just walk away, you're either gonna get beat down every time they see you, or you're gonna get killed," warned Minor, a friend of the group who wore scholarly wire-rim glasses. "That's your choice right there.

"See, gang members aren't looked up to like they were in my dad's day," he continued. "Back then, they were respected for helping the community, helping to build it, 'cause they knew they'd spend the rest of their lives there." Where a neighborhood was once a barrio ("where you grow up with everybody and they take care of each other"), it was now a 'hood ("where you're just protecting your gang").

But Bandit felt gangs had their positive virtues. He provided the usual excuses: A gang supplies love; they're filled with surrogate father figures for youth from mother-centered households; they teach you about the streets and help you earn money through drug trafficking. "Also, they can give you that feeling of superiority, that you're

Gangsta: Merchandising the Rhymes of Violence

better than everything," Minor agreed. "White America says, 'You just join a gang,' like one day you're not a member and the next you're in, but it's not like that. What gangs make you feel is that you can conquer anybody, man, cause you got that backup!"

"If your brother gets killed and he's in a gang and you're not?" Bandit asked. "You gotta go avenge him for him and his gang. That's your brother! That's the guy who took care of you! You gotta go take care of him." After a pause, "He took care of you when you were young, so now you gotta die for him."

Gang culture would never die, they said. The gangs were too embedded in our society and had too many supporters. Unity would never work because people who lost relatives to gang violence would never forgive their enemies. We were now heading for another party, and the sidewalks in Pico were deserted. Big Dave, a quarterback-size teen bodyguard for the group, stopped his car in front of a brightly lit 7-Eleven. Slow Pain withdrew from his own ride and approached us. "Don't worry about it, *vato*," he reassured me. "This is our side." By another car, Bandit flirted with a gaggle of heavily made-up Mexican girls, telling them about his record deal as their eyes sparkled with interest.

Entering the store, we marched down past orderly shelves. In front of the morgue-gray freezers, we debated on whether to buy malt liquor or Budweiser. Since the manufacturers of Bud, Anheuser-Busch, aggressively marketed their product with what Earl Shorris called "an expensive and utterly cynical effort to increase consumption of its products by Latinos" and implied that they loved the "Latino" community through its hiring practices (hiring Latinos for jobs at all levels of the corporation), we purchased four twelve-packs of Budweiser.

As they lugged the cases of beer towards the car, they said we'd be going to a party. They looked like happy elves, scurrying about and sticking close to the beer my *Spin* per diem had paid for.

Our destination was a dark home on an empty quiet road, where another gathering, this one smaller and more casual, was taking place. In another small yard, we approached three women sitting on lawn chairs. Drinking beer from bottles, they listened to oldies songs on a small battered radio. The driveway was dark and their faces were obscured by shadows. In another corner, three Mexican men in khaki and T-shirts held tall-boys and scowled. Slow Pain and Bandit politely introduced themselves to the men then turned to the women. I opened a can of beer and laughed when Bandit turned off the oldies, played a hip-hop tape and began performing one of his songs.

Lil' Vern was a wallflower; he stood by the cases of beer as vigilantly as an usher. I reached for another and asked if he was okay but, in his own world, he gave no indication of having heard.

The impromptu performance ended and Lil' Vern staggered over to the group. Holding another beer, he ranted about how Street Mentality were gonna be large. The Mexican men had seen enough; they put their beers down and left. Our hostess escorted them to the curb and kissed each on the cheek. When she returned, things loosened up. The women asked if I was from New York. Bandit and Slow Pain drank more beer and remembered their dead homiez. Having to always watch your back was a hassle, they admitted. They were wary of Lil' Priest's teenage murderer. No one dared confront him. He had nothing to live for and actually wanted to die in a gunfight. As if disgusted by the sad turn the party had taken, Lil' Vern suddenly moaned, held his stomach and vomited onto the driveway.

Bandit and Slow Pain dragged him away from the house as Vern slurred, "I'm alright," and wiped his hand across his mouth. Our exasperated hostess rose from her seat as her mother opened a window and stared from behind a curtain. Lil' Vern lurched forward again; another clump of vomit spattered onto their lawn.

I woke up the next morning with a hangover and with the hostess next to me in bed. We'd fucked on the floor of my bathroom—missionary position, doggy style, her sitting on top of me on the toilet, in the shower, on the sink—and now she was in bed with me.

Rubbing her round golden ass, I asked her to ride me again. She put her big bronze-colored titties in my face and I kept glancing at my dick poking her jet-black pubic hair. Afterwards we lit cigarettes and she refreshed my memory on the previous evening. We had been speaking on the curb when the Mexican trio returned. They didn't want me speaking with her, they said while surrounding me. "That's my sister!" one of them, her younger brother, yelled. As she tried to pacify him, noting that I had not been disrespectful, Bandit, Slow Pain and, miraculously, Lil' Vern ran up to us. Rushing to his car, Big Dave opened the back trunk and kept one hand near the small arsenal he drove around with. Accepting her decision, that she'd spend time with me, her younger brother left. Big Dave ushered us into his vehicle, patting my back and saying I needn't worry; he would've blasted them before anything happened.

The woman brushed her thick black hair from out of her face. She was a secretary, and tired of fearing the gangs in her neighborhood, but since she couldn't afford to move, what could she do? When she stood up to fix her hair, then reached for the phone to "check in at home," I knew I'd miss her. She ended her phone call and reached for her blouse; the Mexican men had told her husband she was with me at the Hyatt and he had reacted badly. He'd vowed to get his small .22, find her and bring her home. We fucked one final time then she rushed off. After locking the door behind her, I noticed her phone number on my bedside dresser. And her note said, "Call."

Later that afternoon, Bandit spoke of how gangs cast a shadow over his existence, even as he continued acting as he had during his stint with a Blood set. We got into a car and rode down overcast streets, towards the home of a deadbeat who owed Bandit money. He stepped on the gas when we passed a certain avenue, explaining that it was the 'hood of a gang called Pico Nuevo.

"We don't really get along with them," he shrugged. "I had a lot of shit with them, just like Larry [Slow Pain]." The car stopped in front of a suburban home and he rushed out. The teen who owed him money was trying to make it home but Bandit caught him. A second later, Bandit returned to the car. "Damn! That *vato* doesn't have it right now! Drive him down the block to where he gotta get it! I feel I wanna fuck that nigga up right here on the grass!" Entering the car, the frightened teen sat near Minor. "Where we going?" he asked coldly, then began driving. Outside, Bandit feigned anger and waved a huge brown fist in the teen's direction.

Passons Boulevard was a tree-lined suburban neighborhood, the type that your average ghetto kid would describe as their American

Dream — clean streets, trees, slow traffic and sunshine. The only problem were the children.

Most of them rode Big Wheels and tricycles and became the teens who played football for their high school teams; but some became the baby gangsters clad in Pendletons and baggy trousers, who crept slowly down clean, quiet streets in noisy cars, searching for a victim to hit up. The children whose heads you once patted suddenly became the predators you tried to avoid.

Minor sat behind the wheel, staring at the door to the home that the deadbeat had entered. The kid said he'd be right back. We sat in silence. The gentle breeze developed a hard edge. I smoked a cigarette and blew ribbons of morgue gray smoke out of the window. It would be such a peaceful area if the killing would stop. They didn't realize what they had: homes, cars, family. The hum of the engine filled the car.

There was an eerie, still quality to our waiting; it was like a police stakeout gone wrong: The kid had been in there too long. The silence was maddening; the waiting took on an ominous tone. Minor glanced over at me; suspicion blinked from the corner of an eye. This was a quiet neighborhood and the streets were empty, but I felt like Cary Grant stranded in the middle of nowhere, wandering around before an airplane appears to rain hot death from the sky. The door to the house opened slowly. Here it comes, I thought, expecting the worst. The deadbeat was frowning but came out alone, and in his hands he held the money he owed. Everything was alright, I turned to tell Minor, but the graveness of his expression mortified me.

A carload of gangbangers had stopped across the road. Smoke emanated from the car's open rear windows. The car was crowded and the sound of loud music was punctuated by their rowdy yells. The inhabitants were smoking weed, guzzling 40s and challenging us with grinding stares. Forties and weed could turn casual cruising into a spontaneous drive-by, and the car could hasten a post–drive-by escape. "Oh shit," Minor whispered, not even hearing the deadbeat reenter the car and happily note that he had Bandit's loot. "W'sup?" a voice called from the other ride, motionless in front of us, as if its inhabitants were deciding on whether to hit us up or not. Seemed we were in their 'hood. I kept my poker face on and restrained myself from shoving Minor and yelling, *"For God's sake! Get us out of here!"*

62

Gangsta: Merchandising the Rhymes of Violence

"Try not to look at them," Minor said calmly. "We're just gonna leave." He released the brake and drove slowly, without so much as a glance in their direction. None of us said anything. It was a silent drive to the deadbeat's driveway.

The deadbeat hadn't even noticed we were in any danger; he jabbered away at Minor. When he left the car, Bandit quickly snatched him by the back of his shirt collar. "Come here! I gotta talk to you." Dragging him farther from his home he barked, "You're a fucking dick! You should've never did business with me!" It was the oldest scene in the world: the trembling junkie cowering before an angry dealer. "It'll never happen again," he whined, reenacting dialogue familiar to viewers of *Baretta* and *Kojak*.

Disgusted, but paid, Bandit shoved him onto the grass.

"I just threatened his mother," he laughed facetiously, counting the crumpled bills in the car. "They know! I feel no remorse for someone like that! I gotta make money on the side dealing drugs!" Then, in an exaggerated tone: "I gotta 'slang.' " He was performing for the journalist.

Minor laughed nervously. "He tried this shit the other day and I pulled that gun Lil' V had on him today." Entourage member Lil' V carried a small .380.

"I told him, 'You either get me my money or you get dissed!' " Bandit roared.

We rode silently over a small bridge. Underneath it, they said, gangs like Rivera and C.R. occasionally battled it out. "Veteranos, homes," Minor mumbled, "now and then to the death."

Purple-orange skies signaled the approach of night as we drove by Rose Hill Cemetery. Gnarled trees hung over an army of blue-white stones and leaning crosses. On the radio, Keith Sweat begged a woman for her love. It had been a rough day, I reflected; another empty day. "We're heading for the weed spot," Minor mentioned. I stared at the endless rows of graves and wondered why I drank so much.

"My homie Dice was a rapper and got blasted on," Bandit remarked, sobered by the sight of the dead. "He was outside on Larry's porch kicking rhymes with two or three MCs. Three times with a .22. There was blood all over the grass. Ambulance comes up with the shock machine and brings him back. You don't even have to look like a gangbanger to get shot. You just gotta be at the wrong place at the wrong time. But if you tell them you're a rapper with hip-hop they don't really trip too much. They figure you ain't in the shit so everything's cool. They like hip-hop."

We drove into an alley, wearily exited the car and almost bumped into a stocky Mexican O.G. "You going up there?" he said roughly. He didn't wait for a reply; he reached out his hand and handed Bandit a twenty-dollar bill. "Take this money and get me a bag 'cause I can't move my car." Bandit knocked on a door, it opened, he handed the money over, the door closed. A second later, the door opened and a bronze hand quickly passed him two clear pouches of weed.

Bandit bowed his head as if before a ruler and handed the O.G. his bag. The O.G. stared into our faces, searching for dishonesty, then tested the Ziploc's opening strip. Satisfied that no one had tampered with his order, he asked, "You a rapper?"

"Yeah," said Bandit.

"I hope it's none of that yanta shit—" *Yanta* was a word like *nigger*, Bandit told me later.

"It's my lifestyle, that's all—" he told the O.G. with a look in his eyes that said he didn't want any trouble, which asked, "Can I go now?" Glaring until satisfied that Bandit was abundantly fearful of him and what he represented, the O.G. nodded at him, then walked away. The car was utterly silent as we drove down Azusa Avenue, a wide two-lane street that was once the area's cruising strip "until a gang named Puente started hanging here and *la jura* shut it down."

"But you'll never see them unless you go down back alleys," Minor said, "and if you do that, you'll get fucked up."

The thick smoke made breathing difficult; they erroneously believed the *High Times* propaganda about marijuana being healthier than alcohol. We all had our poisons but not even the weed could help them escape the oppressive reality of the gangs.

The O.G. was typical of how other cholos viewed Mexicans in hip-hop, Minor said. "Let's say a gang member was a Blood; if cholos caught him doing that, they'd kill him, just for being a Blood. He's not trying to be Mexican; he's trying to be Black."

Bandit objected scoffingly; idealistic, he hoped unity could prevail. "At the age of seventeen I was a Blood. I was a Mexican with a Black gang," he said for my benefit. "I don't care what color you are: gangs are all the same in terms of love. People love each other if they're in unity."

"But if a cholo heard you talking like that, he wouldn't talk to you because of his pride," Minor sternly reminded him. "That's something deep within us and it does suck."

"—'cause it's racism!" Bandit noted somberly.

During the protracted silence that followed, the last statement hung between them; Minor was of the traditional school of thought while Bandit believed in hip-hop's unifying aspects. To avoid an argument, Minor changed the subject. I watched a police car roll down an empty street as he told a story about two deaf-mute kids: they had been speaking with sign language in downtown L.A. and their sudden hand movements attracted the attention of a passing 'banger, who saw their hands forming letters, pulled a gun and started shooting. "He thought they were throwing *senas*." Minor shrugged his thin shoulders. "They shouldn't have been doing that in public," was the moral of the story. No one was safe anymore; it was all out of control.

Chapter 4

Love and War

"Do not become envious of the man of violence, nor choose any of his ways."

—*Proverbs 3:31*

Mellow Man Ace pulled up outside of the hotel in his maroon 5.0 Mustang just as the sun began to slip out of the clear California sky. He greeted me warmly but I could see a struggle in his face. There was something sad and a little lost in his expression, of youth and suffering side by side, and bitterness made his once hopeful eyes dim and haunted. His wife and child were on his mind, he said, truncating a sigh. I got into the backseat of the car, a prized possession with the words "Straight Ballin'" painted on it. We burned rubber with a deafening screech, then stole silently down half-empty roads. "I'm'a stop by my mom's place," he said. "You could eat some Cuban food. You'll like it. Maybe you can get an interview with my brother's group."

His brother's group was Cypress Hill, the Next Big Thing in the industry, and they had seemed to forget that it wasn't until Mellow put them on his debut album that their career had taken off.

We drove down Hollywood Boulevard, where ten Guardian Angels marched, and listened to Moneymatt's demo for "Watch Your Back." On the freeway, careening past other cars, Mellow released the steering wheel, swung his arms over his head and freestyled—even as the car swerved into another lane and perilously close to other vehicles. "Around my block they don't allow that gang shit," he said passionately, eyes on the road again. "Niggas be buyin' them little cholo bikes and we hit them up: 'Why the fuck you trying to bring that gang-banger shit around here for?' "

In the vicinity of his mother's home, we saw gang members lying on the grass in a park, some of them drug dealers in baggy pants and T-shirts. The mere sight of them caused Mellow's blood to boil. "Look! There go some right there," he agonized. He pointed his finger as if they were animals and this were a safari tour. "The Bishops, they're Bloods; the 9-Deuce Hoover Crips; the Garden View Locs, they're kinda wild—they didn't know we was into this hip-hop thing and they'd try to flip when they'd see us wearing red or blue. Some mornings we'd wake up, throw it on and not give a fuck! The Playboys down this street"—he pointed—"I had some clashes with them years ago," he nodded despairingly. "See, I'm not with the gang scene but I got chased by them gangbangers in Hollywood."

Mellow's DJ FM, recently arrived from Miami, said from the backseat, "They came out and said, '*Que barrio, ese?*' I didn't say nothing and these kids with bats surrounded the car! They hit my boy with a bat and we took off! There was a car of them following behind! I'm from the East Coast. We went through that already. I didn't know what to do when they asked me what neighborhood I was from."

"All this shit started when they formed football teams for their streets to play teams from other streets," Mellow discerned. "When they saw they weren't making no money from the shit, it was a slow process to becoming a gang."

Nearing his mother's neighborhood in the Southgate section, Mellow pointed at a group of men in a parking lot, all of whom wore striped shirts, khakis and black shoes. "All Mexicans," he stressed. "They be throwin' me the finger." He navigated a severe turn. "I'm'a show you some more. It'll only take a minute." We headed down a residential neighborhood and he recklessly pointed out a home, continued driving, brought the car to a screeching halt in front of another and pointed. "This one, Crip little niggas; this blue house, they sometimes go out and throw drive-bys. . . ."

He didn't fear that these 'bangers might take offense and come out shooting.

He drove around a corner, headed down an alley and stopped in front of a deli to buy some beer. As we re-entered the car—him with a can, me with a quart—his Puerto Rican friend Willie limped up. Willie—"who ain't with a gang," Mellow spit—had wobbling legs, the gait of a cripple and a hapless expression on his face. "He was shot in a drive-by four and a half years ago in front of a fucking club," he said. "They were out to kill somebody and just shot into the crowd. We was just chillin'! It was an *ese* [i.e., Spanish-American] gang—"

"The Bloods and Crips got together in the park last week to unite but then the Mexican gangs came and shot everything up!" he lamented. "They figured it was a good way to get everybody they hated in the past at one time." When the shooting was over, four Crips and two Bloods were wounded. "Now the Crips think it was the Bloods that did it. Now there's gonna be some havoc!"

On his mother's block, we sat in the parked car. We saw Muggs and B-Real of Cypress Hill through the front windshield, as if they were on television. They were with their inner circle of friends, and everyone wore T-shirts embossed with the group's macabre logo.

One baldheaded Black youth in the Cypress clique, named Snowman, swaggered around and swung a thick metal chain in his hands. "He's not a gangbanger," Mellow noted with repulsion, "he just busts kids for self!" He recalled the scene of violence. One of Snowman's victims—a long-haired white boy once struck by the cable in his mouth—stood at his attacker's side. "And there they are, just hanging out like nothing happened." The area around the white kid's mouth was stiff. "Wired shut permanently." Mellow shook his head.

Muggs, the group's Italian-American producer, organized his crew for a trip to a local nightclub. Bored, he paced back and forth with a wooden bat in his hands. Swinging the bat, he mimicked hitting an enemy: "In case someone wants to get live," he warned the sky above him.

A car pulled up alongside us, and Mellow was soon engaged in conversation with a stunning beauty. She leaned across her front seat with her black hair in her face and asked how he was doing. Her eyes sparkled with sexual promise, her perfect mouth, covered with scarlet lipstick, smiled and pouted. Mellow said he was fine, that his album would be released any day now and that he had moved to a new apartment in a so-so part of town. "But I got this little piece-of-shit .25 in the house just in case," he chuckled sadly. After laughing, she said she'd love to see him again. He handed her a pen and asked for her number, and for a second his depression seemed to leave him.

But now she promised to call and waved good-bye before driving off. I told him he was a lucky man. Half-heartedly he shrugged, then drank his beer.

Walking towards his former home, he politely greeted one or two of the crew. Inside, he ran towards his two-year-old son, who was named after Desi Arnaz, the first Cuban star in America. He saw his brother heading for the shower but didn't greet him; they weren't getting along too well.

Minutes later, his brother Sen—the loud voice on Cypress Hill's string of hits—was in his bedroom, staring into a mirror and running fingers through his afro. At first he was distant—possibly embarrassed by the wood-paneled walls and bunkbeds in his small room; possibly offended by the intrusion—but then: "My brother says you wanna interview me? Go ahead."

He told me he joined his first gang at the age of fourteen but left because the *eses* couldn't see past his dark Cuban complexion; afterwards he joined Black gangs. But he never had to be a gangbanger, he confessed. "I came from a good family, good home, but I wanted to. I was just attracted to it; and all the girls liked rowdy kids. It was a question of having heart and proving it; and to prove it you had to do shit."

At eighteen, he saw his first homeboy get murdered. "He was a real good friend of mine, twenty-six, and they got him with an M-16 all in his chest. It was the first thing that made me feel I wanna stop 'bangin' but I still kept at it.

"What fucked things up wasn't the dope scene," he reminisced. "It was when crack came in. That's when it wasn't about being together to be against other kids from other places trying to come on your street; that was when everybody said fuck it, and started going for self, to make what they could. Then other gangs from other 'hoods and 'undercovers' got to come in. In one year four of our boys got shot. That took shit out of it for me 'cause these were homeboys that I used to look up to when I was growing up.

"After that I said forget it, and started hanging on my own," he sighed. He met Muggs and started the group, but B-Real, their vocalist, was still involved with gangs. "I knew he wasn't gonna stop until

Gangsta: Merchandising the Rhymes of Violence

he told himself he wanted to." Eventually he did, and the group made their first appearance on Mellow's album; from there, they became stars in their own right, which made it possible for Sen to look back on his gang experience and say, "It's a cycle that you get into and it ends with you getting life in prison or killed. To a kid who wants to get into a gang I'd say, 'Being somebody in life is easier than you think. If you choose the streets, you will end up in prison; and when you end up there, there's no way out.'" He glanced at me as if to ask "All done?" and left the house.

"So how'd it go?" Mellow inquired at the dinner table. We both had plates of rice and steak in front of us, and his moms entered from the kitchen with huge glasses of fruit punch. I said fine and thanked him. He nodded, and turned towards his meal. His sister entered the home and I tried to stare at anything but her. After pecking Mellow on the cheek, she lifted young Desi up in her arms then asked Mellow how he was doing. Slightly depressed again, he said he missed his wife. He didn't go into detail but they were separated.

When his sister and mother left the room, and Desi was out of earshot, I told him to relax, to stop being so hard on himself. "When you came in, your kid right away started singing your song 'Mentirosa.' He knows who you are; he's proud of you. He ain't gonna forget you."

He nodded, still unconvinced. "That's true," he said just as his mother reentered the room.

"I've been trying to tell him that many times," she grieved in Spanish. "But my son doesn't want to listen. If she comes back, she does; if she doesn't, he has to move on."

With a nod, he rose, propelled himself quickly from his seat like a puppet with its strings yanked. He tightly hugged his son, then his mother. Slipping on his jacket, he said we'd be going to a nightclub. Opening the front door, he looked relieved to see the streets quiet at this hour. He walked out into a June night as cold as November. In his car again, I lifted the quart of beer I left in the front seat. The 5.0 crept silently toward the railroad tracks at the end of the block. "Right across there," he narrowed his eyes. "There's this gang that don't dare come over to this side—"

Moving Target

A hot summer Friday afternoon and for some reason Andre Young was wearing an all-black outfit and black wool cap, grimacing as he steered his car around a corner—trying his hardest to look like the urban gangsta he portrayed on his records. "Shit," he said in his best Eastwood tone, facing the bumper-to-bumper traffic on this West Hollywood street. Prostitutes chatted with johns near Grauman's Chinese Theater; tourists peered into shop windows; blinding sunlight bounced off of car hoods; smog obscured the view.

Short Mexican men with bushy hair waved plastic bags filled with oranges at cars waiting for a traffic light to change. Other Mexicans in faded jeans and colorful T-shirts carried huge placards that read MAPS TO STARS' HOMES. Above us, the Hollywood Hills: the "exclusive area" for affluent whites. If someone dropped a cigarette into those heavily wooded forests, their whole shit would go up in flames. The hills evoked thoughts of John Steinbeck's Okies and migrant workers, and the violence that early settlers must have perpetrated against the Indians who lived in California as early as the year 10,000 B.C. California, in fact, was not supposed to exist. This was all really a converted desert, complete with transplanted palm trees.

"This shit'll clear up soon," Dre said, fumbling with the buttons on the car radio. His face was rounder than before he dropped out of sight (after the fiasco at the BRE Convention in New Orleans, where police officers charged Dre with assaulting seven officers, and media accounts connected him to the stabbing of a teenager).

As we sat and waited, I thought about the story I heard on the news last night. A woman got a restraining order against a white man. He didn't let that stop him. As he tried breaking into her home, to exact revenge, she dialed the police. Her call was recorded by 911, and subsequently aired on the news. "He's trying to break in right now," she shrieked. Behind her, the sounds of someone banging on her door. After a loud crash, she began to address the violator. Multiple gunshots. Police eventually caught up to the killer. Pulled him over on the freeway. He burst out of his car in what appeared to be Kevlar body armor, with guns blazing. Over one hundred shots were fired. Police killed him on the freeway.

Adjusting the dial on the radio, Dre nodded to an Egyptian Lover song. Dre followed these electropop records back when he deejayed in various clubs in Compton . . . before he became one of the most successful producers in hip-hop history. "We had a little four-track studio in the back of the [Eve's After Dark] club. We'd go and make our demos during the week and play them on the weekend to see how they would do."

The crowd's positive reaction led to the formation of the World Class Wreckin' Cru, a group best known for their mascara, sculpted Jheri-Kurls, lace gloves, frilly scarves and form-fitting spandex jumpsuits. When Dre reappeared with the group NWA, selling millions of albums with a "gangsta" image, many of NWA's detractors invoked this former image as proof that NWA were poseurs.

Asked about this, Dre almost laughed. *"Ran around like Prince?!* I'll tell you what: I never had no motherfucking lace on. That was Yella. I had some way-out shit on. I was motherfucking seventeen years old. I had some way-out . . . a motherfucking 'doctor suit.' I used to put on a little getup, do a little show . . . That was my little thing. I'd put on a doctor's suit, stethoscope and shit, get up there and mix, you know, whatever. . . . Me? I don't give a fuck 'bout what nobody got to say!"

Thirty seconds later, he was ready for the next question: NWA's beginnings. "Me, Eazy and Ren grew up in the same neighborhood. Well, really, it started off with, um, me and Eazy." Around 115th and Van Ness in Compton. "We wanted to do some shit that was different. The kind of shit that we were doing in clubs." They'd get onstage with X-rated parodies over someone else's record. Run-DMC's "My Adidas" became "My Dick"; high school humor, *Fast Times at Compton High*. "Off of somebody else's beat," Dre repeated, amazed that they once needed tracks. They performed at the Skateland rink, where, during what sounds like a demented night at The Apollo, two thousand people threw things at any group they thought lacked talent. "The place was rowdy as a motherfucker. You had to get up there and get busy. The kind of shit we did on record was what we were doing long before onstage."

As the Wreckin' Cru built a rep, competing with rival group Uncle Jam's Army, Dre felt creatively limited. "I wanted to get up out of that shit. Money wasn't right. Basic reasons. I just felt like I wanted to be in control of my shit. I was just sitting in the studio knowing what I can do . . . just listening to . . . I didn't have . . . have no input on a lot of that shit that came out. I would just give my idea. I wasn't pushing no buttons so I decided, Yo, I'm'a find me a group to produce. I'm gonna find me a motherfucker with some money to back this.

"So what I did is, I went out to Orange County and found a little group. They were fly. They were from the East Coast and, um, I knew Eazy had some money at the time." Dre approached him, and another guy for financing. After playing a tape of the group's music, the other guy backed out. "I'm'a go out here and make me some ends on the street," Dre quoted: "Fuck all this shit y'all talkin' 'bout." Eazy, meanwhile, saw the bigger picture: a partnership with Dre meant money.

Dre called his buddy Ice Cube, who was in a group on the Cru's label, the Stereo Crew, and asked him to ghostwrite lyrics. Cube said "Bet" wrote a song and had Dre pass it to the duo. "They was like, 'Yo man, we ain't doing that song! That's a West Coast record! That's West Coast rap! We ain't doing that shit!' So they left and weren't nobody in there but me and Eazy. Turned out the song was 'Boyz-N-the-'Hood.' That's how Eazy started rapping." At first, a reticent Eazy said, "I can't do this shit!" After much encouragement, a star was born. "He put on his glasses and shit. He did the record, we put it out and sold it out the trunk. About five thousand records, you know, and somebody picked it up. Bam! There it was. . . ."

After NWA's debut album, *Straight Outta Compton*, made them superstars, Ice Cube left the group. Jerry Heller and Eazy underpaid him, he told the press—$32,700 for his contributions to two albums that had combined sales of three million copies. "While their manager Jerry Heller took home $130,000 from the $650,000 their tour made—allowing him to live in a plush house in West Lake—Cube was still living in his mother's house, washing the dishes and taking out the garbage. He had no royalties, no merchandising, no publishing and no contract," wrote *The Source*'s Cheo H. Coker.

"He wanted to do his own thing," Dre said of Cube. "He felt like he wasn't getting treated right and he wasn't, so he said fuck it and got out."

Was there any tension before his official departure? I asked Dre now.

"I felt the shit, you know?" He tried to hide any disappointment or disillusionment, concealing any nostalgia for the early days. "I didn't feel it till he came over to the house one day." Dre had a studio in his home back then, in an upstairs bedroom, and the group regularly assembled there. During one get-together, as Ren, Yella, Eazy and Dre went upstairs and Dre informed Cube they were going to start the session, Cube remained seated on the couch and said he'd sit this one out, that he wanted to watch television.

"So I was like, 'Aw shit.' I knew something was going on." Cube told the group he was out.

His *AmeriKKKa's Most Wanted* debut, produced by The Bomb Squad, would sell over a million copies and establish him as a major hip-hop soloist. "But it didn't affect us," Dre claimed. "It was like this: He was just put in the limelight for NWA. You could have grabbed anybody off the street that could rhyme and could've been a . . . a fuckin' Ice Cube! If you saw how I would direct in the studio, you'd know. I'd sit there and I would punch in, sometimes each line: so and so and so and so, *Boom*. Stop. On Eazy, that's what you had to do 'cause he can't rap! All the way through the song. . . .

"And when you hear it back, it sounds like they just flowed all the way through. So I could've just did that shit with anybody. I taught them how to be, uh, how to work in a studio."

In a separate telephone interview, Eazy confirmed that Dre was indeed the group's Phil Spector—sculpting their raw street tales into easily digestible Pop Chart Material—but added: "I never said I was no hell'a rapper but look at Dre! I never said I could be battling and shit; but I did the record and the shit sold! If you wanna talk about who's

Gangsta: Merchandising the Rhymes of Violence

really from the streets it's me and Ren! What group was Dre in before NWA? World Class Wreckin' Cru with romance and rap and all that other bullshit! What group was Cube in? CIA, and before that Stereo Crew. What group was me and Ren in? None! We were out there doing the shit for real!"

■■

Dre parked the car in front of Snoop Doggy Dogg's apartment building in West Hollywood. "I want you to hear some of the new stuff," he said, inserting a cassette of the album in progress. The first thing I heard was an "Impeach the President" drum machine, coated with Bernie Worrell–like funk synthesizers. The music evoked NWA's "Always Into Something" from their final album, but tighter, more focused . . . From the sound of it, Dre saved his best tracks for a solo album he knew would be inevitable when his relationship with Eazy soured. Snoop's distinct vocals, Slick Rick meets X-Clan's Brother Jay, began insulting Eazy and Tim Dog, Dre's archenemies, saying both needed "a big fat dick."

Then a soundbite from a Blaxploitation flick, a sanctimonious voice preaching, "In order to make this work, we gotta get rid of all the pimps and pushers," was interrupted by Dre's cronies, who yelled, "Nigga, is you crazy?!" The car filled with crashing ride cymbals and high-pitched radar effects; The bass in "Rat-a-Tat-Tat" rattled my chest cavity . . . Dre rhymed over the large horrornoise, threatening his enemies and the average gang-affiliated street kids, his delivery looser than with NWA; Snoop provided a catchy chorus. ("Rat-a-tat-tat / Rat-a-tat like that / I never hesitate to leave a nigga on his back"). Behind the vocal, machine guns blasted—and high-pitched noises— similar to what Terminator and the Bomb Squad threw on Public Enemy's "Night Train," only slower, causing Dre to nod his head then stop. Happy to be playing the album in an official capacity, he pressed FAST-FORWARD and said, "This is my favorite shit right here." The ominous "Mr. Officer" combined Jamaican chatting with a "Deep Cover" bass line.

Dre reclined, stared dreamily out of the window at nothing, nodded and lost himself in the madman's symphony. Horrific noise calmed his soul; the music an external portrait of his emotions. If White America felt "Cop Killer" was bad, I thought, wait till they heard, "Mr. Officer, Mr. Officer, I wanna see you laying in a coffin, sir."

We strolled towards the entrance to Snoop's building and entered, just as Snoop's landlord, an overweight white woman with glasses, called Dre over. "Have you seen him?" she asked. All nervous "aw shucks, ma'am" smile, Dre said no, not for a few days now. . . . "But if I do, do you want me to tell him something?" She stopped, thought about her elusive young tenant. "No, no, I'll run into him eventually." America's best-loved new artist had not paid his rent yet.

At Snoop's front door, Dre reached out his large fist—one allegedly used in so many horrible episodes—and pounded like a medieval barbarian at the castle gates. The door opened and a shirtless Black teen yelled, "W'sup!" In his hand, this stocky kid held a thick butcher's knife. "Oh, it's you." The living room was overfurnished, filled with couches, a coffee table, a TV and stereo system. A piece of paper with the words Dogg Pound was Scotch-taped to a door leading to a bedroom. Another kid (taller, light-skinned and big-armed) walked in, punched Dre in the arm. His hoarse, raspy voice began snapping on the producer. Like an O.G.'s tats, old scars covered this guy's arms, torso and back. This was Trey Curry, alias The D.O.C., whose critically acclaimed, Dre-produced *No One Can Do It Better* yielded the hits "Getting Funky" and "The Formula."

Prior to the car wreck that left him with severed vocal cords, Doc was preparing a follow-up. In Snoop's living room, he threw pointed insults, then sat near Dre on the couch and watched a video by DJ Quick: " 'Born and Raised in Compton' is the bomb," Dre mused. "That's some good shit." But wasn't there rivalry between Compton groups? "Really? That's new to me." The TV volume was lowered as Daz, a new discovery, popped in a cassette of MC Ren's *Kiss My Black Azz* EP. "You heard Ren's shit yet?" Daz asked.

Dre said yes; Ren could have found better beats. "Final Frontier" and Ren's title track were too hectic, he felt. "But that shit 'The Alley' is the bomb. He should have had more stuff like that on there."

The television was on as Ren's tape played. The four inviting beauties in En Vogue appeared. Ren's tape was paused. "Free your mind," the ladies screamed, marching down a fashion-show runway, surrounded by androgynist fashion types and posing guitarists. "That one right there got some good titties," Doc roared. "I used to try to

Gangsta: Merchandising the Rhymes of Violence

get with her in high school before she tried to go with Hammer. I know that girl!"

Unconvinced by Doc's outlandish claims, new vocalist Daz sat back, smiled and puffed on a cigarette.

The door to the bedroom adjoining the living room opened and out came Snoop in all his oversleeping, "just got my deal" majesty: shirtless, groggy, lankier than in the "Deep Cover" video, and yawning. After shaking my hand, he headed for his kitchen and, like a quartermaster taking inventory of the ship's supplies, repeatedly opened and shut the refrigerator door.

Mr. "gauge, my Uzi and my motherfucking .22" (as he described himself on the single) was cooking breakfast, filling the apartment with smoke and the sounds of heavy frying. He set plates, knives and forks on the table and ran water out of the faucet. Doc and Daz leapt up and ran to their chairs at the kitchen table, watching as Snoop set down plates.

Snoop reminded me of the bearded cook in every cowboy movie ever made—the galoot who stirs cans of beans on a campfire then bangs a ladle around a metal triangle, yelling, "Chow time!" as the cowboys scurry, kick up dust and yell, "Yahoo!" It was amazing that Snoop, one of America's new "hard gangsta" icons, would allow me to see him in what some would consider a housewife (or maytag) context.

"Hey, Ronin," he called. "You want a pork chop?" While he was the first rap artist in America to properly pronounce my name, I declined. "You ain't Muslim, are you?" he wondered. "A lot of brothers from New York are. Just wondering," he shrugged, returning to his meal. Dre sat alone on the couch, half watching the TV screen; again deep in thought, a distant expression on his face.

■■■

The entire third floor of the Solarr Records building in West Hollywood was slated to house the offices of Dr. Dre's Death Row record label. Dre, Snoop, Doc and Daz entered the recording studio. Snoop and Doc lit up a joint as two women entered.

The engineer, Greg, walked in. "Ay, Dre, you know what would make me happy? Bringing home a Platinum album." Dre continued adjusting levels on the board.

Daz stepped behind a turntable, faced a wall and started moving a breakbeat forwards and backwards, creating a beat with a snare: "[silence] bap-bap bap-bap." Doc and Snoop extinguished a joint and stepped into the soundproof recording booth; instantly their demeanors changed. They spoke louder. Hunched over his mixing board, Dre moved his hands in every direction: twisting knobs, adjusting levels, checking how much power each track pumped.

"Y'all gotta get crazy on that end," he told the artists, preparing to complete a skit for the new album—*The 20-Sack Pyramid*, a marijuana-themed spoof of an old Dick Clark game show. Joined by Daz, they hummed the show's theme song, an economical way of exploiting its nostalgia value. They wouldn't have to pay sample clearers a penny. During the first take, Dre pressed STOP. He rewound, replayed the tape and listened attentively, making sure all was well. "I got to get that first one," he told himself. His brow uncrossed, he pressed more buttons. "Okay, now this time whistle it. If you laugh, fuck it. We'll do it like that."

"So who's gonna be Dick Clark?" Doc joked, not knowing that underneath Dre's easygoing, devil-may-care facade lurked the soul of an agonized perfectionist intent on creating a flawless album that would sell millions and maintain his status as one of hip-hop's top producers. The drum intro from Joe Tex's "Get Out My Life, Woman" played—hardly an original foundation but one that, like "Impeach the President," always seemed to enthrall hip-hop listeners—and the trio resumed their whistling. In mid-take, Dre rudely stopped recording. "Damn, we gotta do that again," he told the performers, who were befuddled, no idea why that take was unacceptable.

Dre's eyes tensed. Oblivious to his surroundings, total attention on the music hitting him in the face, emanating from the studio monitors positioned directly in front of him. Knowing what sounds would work had made him wealthy.

At this point, Snoop, Daz, Korrupt, Rage and all of the other Death Row or Dogg Pound members represented more than Dre's attempt to create a Juice Crew stable of moneymaking crowdpleasers. For Dre, they were his secret weapons, his revenge on NWA. The duo hummed as he hit RECORD. A second later, silence: "One more time," he said, leaning into the microphone on the mixing board. "Fuck, man," Snoop yelled in frustration. RECORD. More whistling. Another false start. "Now hum it," Dre commanded, more intensely, sighting the undefinable element he hoped to capture on tape. Finally, the performance, no different than any given today; but to Dre's ears and mind, something inexplicable was present.

"That's good, right?" asked Snoop, raising his chin and approaching, ready to plop down and enjoy his high until Dre summoned him back into the booth.

After putting another reel of tape onto a recorder as large as a washing machine, Dre handed me a sheet of paper: his personal production notes, scrawled in blue ink, filled with a number of intentional misspellings. "You can write about them if you want," he said, reseating himself in front of the board. "Now we need a small crowd," he muttered, reaching for a disc labeled YOUNG WOMAN (*sic*) AND CHILDREN.

As two women returned from the store with liquor, an engineer named Eric played selections from breakbeat albums and Dre leaped into *Name That Tune* mode. "Aw, that's 'Fuck Tha Police.' The first one." Another break caused Doc to question who used it for a well-known hit. "Just Ice," Dre answered, watching as Doc and Daz began spitting lyrics from BDP's "My Philosophy."

The studio filled with female vocalists and bottles of hard liquor. Dre, the Black Jay Gatsby, with lazy and watery eyes, relaxed with a couple of drinks and scanned the new scene he had built around himself. Sexy women with bulging tits and voluptuous asses laughed raucously, splashing Hennessy into plastic cups; teenagers sat on a couch and argued over who had the 'bomb' lyrics; others lit up thick joints; a burly hanger-on popped in to ask Dre if he needed anything else, and to get a progress report on the album.

The studio, indeed the entire floor of the small building, was what Dre had always wanted. Yet, sitting there in front of the board, staring at a drink in front of him, he didn't seem entirely happy. The room grew noisier, and more people materialized, snatching joints and drinks and flashing gang signs on their fingers. "West Side!" A minute later, Dre spoke with a shapely beauty in a revealing outfit. Daz stood near a keyboard, plunging fingers into keys, creating ominous riffs that Dre would later ask Daz to play on one of his songs.

With glassy eyes, he stared at a teen flashing gang signs, yelling "East Side" at me. " 'Ay! 'Ay! Y'all leave that shit alone! We gonna get

Ronin fucked up!" I hadn't wanted to drink, but the studio session had become a party. Sipping on a gin and juice, I glanced at the production notes: "Fuck With Dre Day," "Nuthin But a G-Thang," "The Day the Niggaz Took Over" and "Rat-a-Tat-Tat."

The room filled with curses, insults, sexual propositions. A crate of records near the 1200 turntable held the records he used. For a second, I thought about sifting through them, discovering his secrets. A hefty woman splashed liquor into cups. Dre instructed her to bring me another drink. "They call me Hennee Loc," she slurred.

"Her tits are so big she could knock you out by slapping you on the head with one of them," Doc cackled.

A grave Dre remembered his mission—would he really be wasting studio time on this sottish interlude if he were with his old group? He had a solo album to complete, didn't he?—and surrounded by what could only be called self-indulgent imbecility, Dre continued recording: RBX and Rage had yet to lay down vocals for the posse cut he thought of calling "Lyrical Gangbang." A plodding beat boomed from speakers, everyone else snapped out of it. Waves of embarrassment passed over their faces: they had made asses of themselves and disturbed their sovereign. After accidentally spilling his drink on the $750,000 mixing board, Doc yelled "Shit!" and Hennee, rubbing circles in his shoulder with her palm, asked, "You okay?" As liquid ran towards danger zones, about to seep into expensive circuitry, Dre leaped up, muttered curses to himself and watched his guests scurry to find a towel. "Or a rag! Get something!"

Things were out of hand: equipment was being fucked with. Doc laughed, apologized and the partying moved to a rehearsal space down the hall, where, slumped over the rear of a plastic seat, Snoop faced innumerable reflections of himself in mirrors lining the walls. "Check this out! This is the chair dance!" he said, seated but walking the chair across the room.

In another corner, Rage moved her sleek legs and heavy bottom in a catlike dance for an appreciative Dre, who sat in front of her, clutching a drink.

Doug Young, an independent record promoter, appeared with a guest: an extremely nervous DJ Mark the 45 King, who heard about Dre's new label and hoped to collaborate with the Death Row artists.

Shaking his hand, Dre led him back into the recording studio. The entourage trailed behind. Mark looked thinner, sweating but no one mentioned it. He popped in a cassette, his latest project for Warner Brothers. Dre raised the volume. Mark nodded to his tambourines, to chanted lyrics. His two female MCs asked, "Who stole the cookies from the cookie jar?" Dre's crowd frowned and commented on how trivial it sounded. The tape was stopped mid-song and Dre said, "Here," handing it back to a slightly puzzled Mark. "Check this out," Dre said, playing the album-in-progress, satisfied, followers nodding and singing along. "Damn," Mark said, clearly embarrassed and defeated. "I'm gonna have to go remake my entire album." He was led out, right past the crate that held a copy of Mark's earlier classic, *Master of the Game*, one of Dre's bigger influences.

Finally, Dre led me into an unlit office, pointed at a chair, said, "You can sit down." He sat behind a large desk. In the window behind him, the California skies turned as purple as a contusion.

"Do you know you come off as being somewhat of a cynic?" I asked, starting the recorder, feeling like Christian Slater in *Interview with the Vampire*.

"Nope. Ask anybody that's walking, 'What are you doing every day?' Doing something to make some fucking money."

"You don't seem to give a shit about anyone. You always talk about wanting to shoot anything that moves. Why are you like this?"

"Just where I ran around at when I was a kid, that's all. The environment, my neighborhood, you know. I lived in a little area they used to call Wilmington Arms when I was a kid. This was in Compton. I lived in like a whole bunch of neighborhoods in Compton. In Blood neighborhoods, in Crip neighborhoods. My grandmother is in a Blood neighborhood. I went to a Blood high school and a Crip high school, but I never got involved with that shit. I think my thing was, 'If you ain't gonna make no money out of it, don't do it.'

"I couldn't see the logic behind doing that shit. Gangbanging's not gonna bring in no motherfucking money. It's just gonna get you motherfucking shot at; you gonna shoot at some motherfuckers; you gonna end up in jail, dead, something like that. It's gotta bring in some motherfucking money."

I tested the waters, mentioned Dee Barnes' name.

"Fuck *Pump It Up*," he said. "They could 'pump up' these nuts!"

To him, Dee Barnes was "another one that's out to get paid. I knew she . . . she knew she had fucked up, so she started saying, 'It wasn't me, it wasn't me!' I saw her and . . . Damn! What happened after that?

"Oh! I was walking over to her and I got ready to talk to her. Somebody came, got in between us, was pushing me back. . . . My boy that was with me hit him. *Bing!* 'Get your hands off of him.' That kid got hit; broke his tooth. He got his tooth broke for getting in the fucking way. I couldn't even tell who it was!" Dre said, restraining a smile, right before a slip-up. "I almost fucked up Ed Lover!

"I was like, 'Yo man, what you doin'! What you doin'!' That kid was like, 'Yo Dre! Dre! Dre!' I was like 'Oh okay,' 'cause it was real dark in there. Then the kid rushed me up out of there. Next thing I know, Dee Barnes called me up on the telephone, right, the very next day, saying, 'Yo, that shit was fucked up what happened, that shit was fucked up.'"

According to Dre, she said, "I ain't gonna press no charges or nothing like that."

To which he replied, "You ain't gonna press no charges for what?"

"She said she had to go to New York to film the show," Dre continued. "She left the very next day. Next thing I know I'm getting a call from her again, saying she's gonna take me to court. If I don't want her to, I have to do three songs for her, something like that. I think it was three songs without putting my name on it and they would forget about it. What?! I start thinking, I ain't do shit! But just to keep the motherfucking air clean, I'll put together some shit. 'Fuck it, get back with me and we'll see what's up.' So I finally start talking to a couple of people; they were like, 'She can fuck you up, you know, because the shit that went on.' I was like 'Fuck it.' "

"I talk to her again," he continued. " 'Fuck it, I'll do the song.' They send some contracts down saying what was gonna happen. I get another call after the NWA album came out—right after the record went number one, maybe two days after that. . . . 'Fuck it! I don't want the songs! I want a million dollars!' 'What?! Fuck you. Take me to court.' Next thing I know the shit is in every motherfucking newspaper there is and I'm in court. I was like 'Damn!' "

NWA's *Niggaz4Life* debuted at number two on the *Billboard* Top Pop Albums chart. A week later it knocked Paula Abdul out of the number one spot. Dre was now viewed as a rich man, and Dee, he felt, wanted money.

As he struggled to suppress a smile, I asked, "Are you in a state of denial?"

"I didn't do shit!" he claimed. "I didn't touch her ass!"

"What was the nature of your relationship with Dee Barnes before the incident?"

"We was cool. We used to hang out, go out and shit . . . me, her and her homegirl."

"Were you ever romantically involved?"

"So-so . . ."

"You knew each other 'pretty well'?"

"Yeah, real well," he laughed, rubbing his chin.

"And how did you separate?"

"It was friendly, 'cause if it weren't, we would have never did that interview in the first place. We weren't doing many interviews back then. We were like, 'Dee, we gonna do this shit then *Bam Bam Boom*, I'm being accused of assault.'"

> *"Confused, yo, but Dre's a nigga with nothing to lose"*
> — *Dre on NWA's "100 Miles and Running"*

Many people thought that Dre beating on wispy Dee Barnes was undeniably foul. Beating on any woman, in fact, was a despicable practice. No one, save for Eazy or DJ Yella, seriously considered that Dee Barnes was at fault. Many hip-hop newspapers, magazines and television programs remained silent, however, fearing that Dre and his boys would seek retaliation.

Only Tim Dog, from the South Bronx, openly took Dre to task for the incident, suggesting on his single "Fuck Compton" that if Dre could beat Dee Barnes, what would stop him from doing the same to his girlfriend Michelé?

I mentioned this to Dre, who fumed at the mention of Tim's name: "Tim Dog?" he asked, mildly skirting the issue. "He's a punk motherfucker that has no motherfucking talent, either! He had to say my name to sell some records. The only songs that you know about a Tim Dog are the ones he's saying my name in." Then, out of the blue: "The most popular song on the last Ice Cube album is talking about me, about NWA! That should tell people something."

How about the "Los Angeles record producer incident" in *Spin* . . .

"Busted him up with my hands?" Dre asked, wide-eyed, arresting another smile. "I'm'a tell you what happened in that episode. . . ." Dre was visiting a friend in her home, he began. So he was leaving her home, and she was walking him out when she saw this guy. "He slept with her niece . . . something like that, so, one day, I was over there kicking it, came out, getting ready to get in the car and leave and she saw him pulling up. She hit the motherfucker! She hit this kid!"

This was hard to believe since *Spin* reported that the victim had sustained broken ribs, a broken jaw, had been beaten up pretty badly. "Next thing I know this kid's saying I hit him, broke his jaw and all this kind'a shit! I figure as hard as a motherfucker works to make his money, there's always somebody out there working just as hard to take that shit away. Always!" He sighed. "Damn, everybody's trying to get paid. All this shit was falling right at the same time, too."

I told him there was more I'd like to discuss. For one, his house burning down. Was it that he was having a "drunken barbecue," as many said?

"I'm'a tell you what happened with that incident," he said. "I don't know how the fire started. This is what the fireman's saying—some motherfucking electrical problems with the air-conditioning." According to Dre, he was having a barbecue with his friends in the *back* of his house while the fire was starting out front. "One of the neighbors came over and said, 'Yo, the side of your house is on fire!' We went over there and put it out. Next thing I know, it was on the roof!" While he lost his home, and didn't expect to have it repaired for "eight or nine months," he had good news: "I'm insured. It was like $250,000 damage."

IV

"NWA's Dr. Dre and four other men were arrested after a fight in a New Orleans hotel in which a fifteen-year-old fan was stabbed. The New Orleans District Attorney's Office is deciding if charges of criminal damage, resisting arrest, battery of officers and inciting a riot will be pressed after four police officers were also injured in the altercation."
—Rolling Stone, *"Notable News," July* 1992

Gangsta: Merchandising the Rhymes of Violence

"The New Orleans thing? That shit got pumped so out of hand," Dre sighed again, preparing yet another yarn about how things just happened to happen to him. In this incident, he was with his boys in a hotel lobby, minding his own business as usual, discussing the Eddie Murphy film *Harlem Nights*. "You know the part where the kid stutters? It's like, 'Come Friday night, I'm knocking somebody the fuck out!' " He referred to a scene when a prizefighter approaches gambler Eddie Murphy at a restaurant table and reassures Eddie that it's safe to bet on him. "These kids overheard us saying that shit, right? So they walk up to us, just out of nowhere, and say, 'Yo, I bet you can't knock my homeboy out right here.' Talking to my boy. . . ." In Dre's version, his boy tried to make peace, telling the troublemaking local, "Go on with that shit. . . . Get out of here!"

"So the kid walked up on him and my boy pushed him back. He walked up again so my boy hit him. *Bam!* And all this shit broke out. They start coming at us. *Boom!* We got in a little tussle and uh, and uh, I start heading for the front door! Police grabbed me—Boom! Boom! Boom!—throwing me in there. I'm like: 'Well, yo, what y'all grabbing me for?' Heh heh.

"They saying I beat up seven police and I incited a riot and some other shit they said I did. I was like, 'Damn, that ain't saying much for your motherfucking police force if I beat up seven police.' "

Then came the accusations that Dre was somehow involved in the stabbing of a fifteen-year-old. "I'm like 'What?!' I ain't even know nothing about that shit. I didn't see nothing like that. Matter of fact, we got the shit on videotape. This kid from New Orleans sent us a video of the whole episode. It has me on videotape—it doesn't have how it started—but it has me going to the door, then you hear a big ruckus. Yo, man, I didn't do jack!"

Eazy-E was preparing to launch a multimillion-dollar lawsuit against Dre. He watched Dre from afar. I asked Eazy his opinion of New Orleans. "He had that Dee Barnes thing, breaking that kid's jaw, driving his car off the cliff, getting shot, New Orleans," he sighed. "None of that shit ever happened to him when he was down with us." But New Orleans? "None of us were there. He was with Doc and that other kid he hangs with." No one would say who this "other kid" was.

In September 1992, *Rolling Stone* wrote, "NWA's Dr. Dre was shot in mid-July. According to Jerry Heller, the group's manager, Dre was shot four times in the leg. Heller said he believed the shooting occurred in South Central Lost Angeles."

Dre denied this as well. "Yeah? How long ago was that? I got shot how many times? Hmmm. They say I got shot four times in the leg?" he joked. "Walking pretty good, huh?"

So you didn't get shot? "I don't remember that shit, though." I repeated the question. "Uh uh. Huh heh heh. Oh shit. Oh shit. [Pause.] Shot at." Really? I'm not trying to call you a liar but . . . "Oh shit!" he laughs. "I got shot at a whole bunch of times. They never reported it before, though. It's funny how all that shit is happening at the same time. Heh heh heh. Funny shit." After a pause, he said, "That incident happened like this . . . We was talking 'bout this girl that came up for one of my homeboys and she was all fucked up . . . uglier than shit . . . So we came downstairs to talk about her, right? Shots rung out. We ran back into the hotel. I don't even know where they came from. And that's that." But the story was in *Rolling Stone* and other magazines. "Like I told you! They called my mom's house. All this *Spin, Rolling Stone, Rap Masters* with what's-'er-name . . . Kate Ferguson? All of them were calling! I was like 'Yo, I ain't got nothing to say to y'all.' "

Eazy-E maintained that Dre had been shot. "Yeah. I don't know exactly where it happened but he got shot four times in the leg. How many people you know get shot four times?" Eazy launched into a speech about "the people Dre's with now," stopping short of saying that his new friends were servants of the devil. Then he said, "When NWA would go to New Orleans, we'd have our passes and be cool about shit. We wouldn't barge in and get into no shit like that! Dre's into something he can't get out of!"

How? Musically? Personally?

"In every way. He's got people that don't know shit about the music business filling his head with all this shit, telling him he could be this, be that, get this, get that . . . But fuck that! I'll show his contract in public and compare it to those of other producers. Nobody was ever robbing him!"

I reminded Eazy of how two members of NWA accused him and manager Jerry Heller of underpaying them.

"Everybody in NWA got paid! Overpaid! Nobody got robbed. It's just that they got people telling them shit in their ear, telling them they could do this, do that. Dre, one of the best producers in hip-hop—since the last NWA album, he ain't done nothing but that 'Deep Cover' single."

Dre, however, insisted that he had been underpaid. "Jerry Heller," Dre spit. "Motherfucker comes in and, uh, pulls Eazy to the side and says 'Look, what you do, you pay him a certain amount of money. I'll draw up the contracts for production and you could be making all this money right here for owning the company!'

"And you know, I'm thinking, Okay this the homie, I'm'a trust him," Dre continued. "But it turned out like that. I shouldn't have. I should've been a motherfucking gangster in the situation."

Eazy denied this; he wanted people to know Jerry Heller was honest. "He's like a father to me! Jerry's cool! If he wasn't, I wouldn't have him working for me. I don't have no partners. I own Ruthless by myself but everybody will come out and say, 'Fuck Jerry Heller!' Jerry Heller works for me! It's that a lot of niggas bring up the black-and-white thing. They don't like Jerry 'cause he's Jewish and shit so they'll be like, 'Oh! He's gonna rob you, he's gonna steal this!' That's that black-white shit from people that don't know shit about the music business or contracts."

But Dre disagreed; it wasn't racism. He felt underpaid. "I think Eazy sucking Jerry's dick or vice versa. Something's going on. It's got to be one of them's fucking one of them. It's no way I'd let a motherfucker come in and break up me and Doc."

While *Rolling Stone* was quoting Eazy-E as saying that NWA would reform "in March," Dre told me they'd do so without him. "When I left Ruthless, I took the sound with me. Everything from now on ain't gonna do what it's supposed to." Hours of talking about his life made him melancholic. From now on, he vowed, he'd stay behind the board, developing newer talent and providing tracks. As a sideline, to protect himself, he would invest in real estate. He wanted a calm life. He was tired of negative press. "I'm a motherfucking calm, laid-back motherfucker," he assured me. "I don't talk that much around people that I don't really know. I like eating motherfucking hamburgers. A laid-back down-to-earth motherfucker. I like kicking it with women, my homies—just chillin', just having a good time."

"But is there a violent side to you?"

"There can be," he nodded. "Yep, there definitely can be, but I try to stay away from those kind of situations now. I done sat down with a couple of older people that talk to me. It's like, 'Look, you can't do the shit you used to do. You can't go to the party with your mother-fucking homies and just hang out, party on the dance floor and kick it.' I'm like, 'Yo, you right! Everybody out there is trying to figure out a way to get some fucking money!'

"They know you got some fucking money," he continued warily. "They know they don't have none so they gonna try to figure out a way to get some from you." He claimed that in the future he would spend more time at home or in the studio, hanging with his friends in a controlled environment and completing the recording of *The Chronic*. "People could say what the fuck they wanna say about me," he blurted out. "But all that shit ain't gonna stop me! I'm'a do what I'm'a do regardless. Just put down, 'Buy the motherfucking records, enjoy them and shut the fuck up!'"

Chapter 6

Japanese Basketball

Many people consider Luther Campbell an extremely lucky man. By his early thirties, he was practically a millionaire. He got paid for rapping about sex and got to make a fortune without having to resort to wearing a suit and tie. In fact, when I first saw him standing in the middle of Narita International Airport, near a pile of luggage, he was wearing a colorful leather Luke Records jacket, jeans and sneakers. It was sundown in Tokyo (population 11,618,281) a city on the island of Honshu, the capital of Japan.

By his side, three Japanese club promoters discussed the itinerary. A dancer stared at arriving passengers. The editor of *Crap Sheet* showed me one of his articles in the current issue. It was a Run-DMC feature that said Joseph Simmons was DMC. "Man, the first time I was here, shit was like a culture shock," Luke interrupted. He shook my hand like a politician.

"How was your flight?"

"Long but bearable," I responded. Fourteen hours of numbing boredom, travel magazines and sanitized in-flight movies.

"That's good! We're just waiting for my dancers to get here with the bags then we're going to the hotel."

When the *Crap Sheet* editor expressed contempt for *The Source*'s TLC cover, I turned away. While I agreed that it was a mainstream sellout, the white college kids at *The Source* made all of the cover decisions.

I asked Luke about the incidents: at shows in New York (The

Apollo) and here in Japan, women leaped onstage, yanked down his zipper and fellated him. "It started out with me just dancing with them, then they start tugging on my shorts," Luke laughed, miming dance steps. "So I'm like, 'Oh you wanna play that?' Man, last night, there were two of them doing it!

"Then there was that show at The Apollo," he says, feigning helplessness. "They ain't gonna stop!"

He sighed and gazed at the crowd brushing past. "I gotta do a radio show, let them know I'm here. You should see the questions they ask over here. First time I got here, They were saying, 'How big is your dick?' On the radio! They had these three famous models and they were asking me, 'Which one would you like to fuck? This one, this one or this one—' They made the shit into a contest, telling people to call in and decide.

"Over here, there's this magazine that has readers writing in for advice on how to fuck their girls. 'Should I eat them or fuck them?' They fax shit over and I answer," he said, a regular Ann Landers. If he was too busy, one of the demure Japanese women in the office jotted down a few fantasies.

"How do you feel about the media's take on you so far?" I asked, this being my only direct question on the trip.

"Man, they always write the same story. I don't wanna talk about censorship all the time. All those magazines ask the same questions. They never wanna write about that other shit: about new albums, influences . . . you never see that."

The Japanese promoters quickly pushed the steel cart loaded with bags, halting traffic for a second as they sped across the street towards a waiting van, where Luke's other dancers stood shivering in the cool night breeze. Bundled up in jackets, they looked short, unremarkable, save for their long hair and gleaming blue eyes. Crossing the street, inhaling cool air and exhaling mist, Luke stared at the sea of colorful neon lights illuminating the jet-black night. "I told myself I'm'a cool out this time around, that I wasn't gonna fuck no Asian bitches. Now I see them out here so I got to do my duty." He had, after all, been referring to himself as Captain Dick in America's music press.

"On the radio, they asked me did I ever fuck an Asian woman. I said, 'Naw but I'm gonna before I leave this motherfucker!'" The ultimate American settler, he had arrived in a new land, seeing not its

Gangsta: Merchandising the Rhymes of Violence

people's rules and regulations so much as their resources to exploit for personal gain. Like the savage bloodthirsty Moors who invaded Spain, ravaged the women and sired the various Latino races, Luke was here in Japan for wine, women, song and as much treasure as he could cart back to his native country.

Immediately, his demeanor changed. From the hedonistic Captain Dick (Super-Barbarian), he had become Mr. Luther Campbell, distinguished businessman and financial advisor on the Japanese Yen. "Watch out for these," he advised, fingering silver coins in *Crap Sheet*'s palm, speaking as delicately to him as the master did to young, bald Kwai Chang Caine on *Kung Fu.* "You might spend these like nothing but they're like one hundred dollars or some shit."

At ten P.M., Tokyo time, Luke had to announce his arrival on a radio interview. Afterwards he would put in an appearance at NHK, the national television station and perform a few songs for the camera. Already running behind schedule, he said, leaping into the van and leaving. But not before he dispatched one of the promoters to put *Crap Sheet* and me into a car, where we sat for an hour, driving past business towers, tons of neon signs for camera film and canned soda, American-styled hotels named The New Yorker, and murky black rivers—until we reached the Shibuya district.

Later that night, Luke's Japanese interpreter Itomi adjusted her black miniskirt over her shapely ass and leaped into the front seat of another car. Moving in beside Luke's dancers, she told the driver to take us to NHK. With her eyes on the dark black road ahead, on the occasional colorful light or dense wooded area filled with ominous silhouettes of tree limbs—where centuries ago, noble samurai fought their wars—Itomi began to detail the ascendance of modern hip-hop music and style into mainstream Japanese youth culture. "They're catching on, I think," she said of the multitude of b-boys storming nightclubs.

"They're going in for the fashion, wearing those caps, sneakers, T-shirts, long shorts. Many kids think hip-hop is a very Black culture so they tan themselves; they go to tanning salons and perm their hair very strong to look like a brother. The language barrier is the only thing that gets in the way. They learn some words but they can't really understand."

After Run-DMC and the Beastie Boys toured Japan in the early

1980s, youth began wearing the Adidas footwear, Volkswagen medallions, sheepskin coats and Kangol hats. When house and techno music arrived—new genres with their own accompanying modes of dress and ritual—most hip-hop listeners leaped on that and hip-hop seemed to be dying. Until Bobby Brown.

"For the general public, what really put hip-hop on fire was Bobby Brown's 'Every Little Step You Take,'" said Ikuko Hirasawa, a woman seated to my left in the backseat. Nervously smiling, she asked Itomi to translate: Ikuko was an editor at *Crossbeat*, a monthly that printed syndicated articles on hip-hop, including my work with *Spin*. "That became the [theme] for an aesthetic salon," Itomi translated. "They used the song on TV and that's how it went to the public in '88 or '89. It wasn't really rap but as far as getting back into Black culture, that started it."

MC Hammer was large out here, she added. "He also brought out the fad of rap, being Black and macho.

"They used to have a variety show on TV, a high-school dance contest, and this is where the kids would make up their own dance routines. They would do what they saw Black people doing in American videos, but adding their own little touches to it."

From this exposure, the cult of modern b-boys who called themselves "brothers" listened to more extreme groups like Public Enemy and NWA, watched *A Rage in Harlem* and the films of Spike Lee, cheered for Michael Jordan and Charles Barkley, wanted to be Mike Tyson, drooled over Robin Givens, bought imported hip-hop gear and darkened their skin. Youth sought their identities in a Black American music culture, clinging to hip-hop's more superficial aspects and consciously overlooking its political intentions. "They don't even understand the words," Itomi groaned. "All they are in it for is the beat, something to dance to. I think half of the kids doing it are trying to understand Blacks and that's why they texture their hair. More than half of them just think that the hair and tanned skin looks good but a lot of the Japanese rap artists are ridiculous, the way they think their dances are good and nice. I think they're getting things wrong because they were going into it backwards."

"The Japanese kids who get into hip-hop are not the studious type," Ikuko continued. "They do not read books, even the people who read

Crossbeat are rock fans who got into the music. They are mostly high school kids and sports fans who are catchy on fashion or trends to follow. They are active kids who have to know how to dance."

"Japanese rap may not sound too good because we have nothing to talk about," Itomi said a bit cynically. "Culturally we are also not the people to protest. There is a sense of apathy. No one cares about anything over here."

"We do not have the social problems America has," Ikuko objected. "It is not that there is not anything to rap about, it's just not something that would be able to fit into the rap way. We have many traditions but how can you rap about it? There was a rapper in the 'old days,' when Japan occupied Okinawa. An Okinawan would be able to rap about this. To other Japanese rappers, I would say the same thing that the American artists have told me: You should not rap about anything you have not experienced. All American rappers say you should rap the truth, but in this country, it's really hard, because everything is so vague." People seemed to be complacent, humble conformists, she elucidated, who expressed gratitude for good or bad.

"I feel Japanese people don't really expose their character," Itomi continued, signaling a quicker route to the cab driver with a pointed finger. "They shake hands and smile but they don't really tell you what they feel. Kissing ass is all they ever do. Also, we don't have many racists in Japan. Your hip-hop movement was aroused by the racial troubles you have every day. This we do not have.

"As we have the upsurge in our economy, it kind of relieves the minds of people. Their minds are free. They're going into a lot of the sexual things as well; and all that fits together with the rap culture, the Black culture. If we believe in certain things, we do them. Whatever is cool or catchy makes everyone jump on the wagon."

The crowded tiny cab rolled up to the imposing NHK Television complex. The other cars were already there. In a playful, alcohol-induced mood, Luke began insulting everyone around him; his voice as raspy as Redd Foxx's, his language as blue. His eyes were hazy, watering, reflecting light. His huge bearded shadow, the bodyguard Ron May, led the way as we marched single file through a parking lot. The dancers admired the fleet of expensive cars, all similarly black and shiny, parked alongside one another. The executives at this station were obviously well salaried—but Luke, who could afford any in the lot, was unimpressed. His dancers remained bug-eyed at the sight of such opulence.

We entered the building and strolled down brightly lit corridors that reminded me of low-budget sci-fi flicks or Riker's Island, and entered the greenroom area. Luke pulled out the nightly fifth of Bacardi, nightly on this tour at least, and proceeded to hold court. "Who's this playing right now?" he asked. ADOR's "Let It All Hang Out," a Pete Rock production with the same track heard on Pete's immensely popular "T.R.O.Y.," the same sugarsap horns and Sly Stone drums. "What label they on?" Luke asked, forehead crinkling with financial interest. Mercury Records, I thought. His face calmed. "See, if they would've signed with me, I'd have it out there like it's supposed to be! Shit! I'd take it down to the Pac Jam and tell them, 'You play this!' Shit would be number one!" He made himself sound like the Mayor of Miami, like an underground Boss Hogg: a powerbroker who called the shots in his town's rackets. His autobiography, *As Nasty As They Wanna Be*, alluded to his earliest days around gangs, and his associates in the "Ghetto Style DJs."

We entered a huge multicolored chamber that evoked memories of the Spanish-channel variety shows my late mother enjoyed on Sunday evenings. Large cameras were posted in strategic spots. A small stage area held a table, with two Technic 1200 turntables awaiting DJ Mike Fresh's arrival. Cameramen and production assistants lounged around; a soundman tested sound effects that would unexpectedly punctuate the taping of the *Doki Doki Shichau* program.

Japanese label reps for Luke's Nippon distributor Teichiku Records watched Luke regally walk across the room and mount the stage. Tomo, with the Peter Frampton hairdo and Luke jacket, pretended to be overjoyed at seeing Luke again. Cameras swirled frantically about the room, bizarre angles foreordained. Production assistants herded the studio audience into a corner. Lethargically, Luke paced the stage, chitchatting with Ron and not taking this seriously.

In shabby costumes, his dancers burst onstage and simulated fornication to a frenetic, slightly generic Miami Bass track—an uptempo, high-hat–heavy groove that sounded like someone programmed a beat, accidentally sped up the tempo and walked away. Nothing too special, just a fast repetitive track styled after Kraftwerk

Gangsta: Merchandising the Rhymes of Violence

or Afrika Bambaataa's "Planet Rock" filled with pleonastic break-beats. This mindless music had made a former chicken fryer wealthy. The music, and his exploitation of women like Desire, the lion-maned, weave-wearing Black beauty who furiously swiveled her thighs and pumped her crotch forward as if interacting with a ghostly penis, tells it all.

Luke's male dancers, themselves C-list Scoob and Scrap imitators, sandwiched her and began humping. Spinning in circles to meet both crotches, she combed her nails through long straightened hair, then bent over, providing the camera with a sumptuous closeup of her g-stringed posterior.

To the audience, Luke cast a redoubtable presence, towering over the shorter Japanese film crew like Godzilla over the Japanese Army in the Toei epics. For a minute the music stopped and Luke stood there, considering the absurdity of it all, surveying the pink, green, black and yellow stage, as well as the cheap-looking 2 Live Crew banner over his head. "Pee-wee's Playhouse," he muttered, laughing to himself, countering the film crew's polite applause with epithets.

A cacophony of foreign voices filled the room as all present said Lord-knew-what about who—Michael Crichton's worst nightmare! Two production assistants smirked as Luke, reveling in the unAmerican freedom from censorship, repeatedly yelled, "Pop that pussy!" His words began to slur; the liquor was catching up to him.

Luke's face tightened under some internal strain, he dipped, grabbed his crotch and nodded his head to the side, performing a heavy-metal headbanging move sideways. The more the tip of his long stocking cap pirouetted, the more he resembled a Christmas elf. "That's the way!" he yelled, a Druid casting spells. "Git it git it," this drunk rapping Black Dionysius roared, his inhibitions as diminished as the fifth of Bacardi in the green room.

The opening act—Japan's Crazy A—swaggered in and stood directly in front of the stage, their hatred for Bass music evident in their faces. They spun on their heels and marched over to a corner, where they huddled, glanced back over their shoulders at Luke's freak show, then resumed their plans on how to blow the talentless American group out of the water. Their manager, a business-minded Buddhist in traditional robe and sandals, followed, his tightly gripped briefcase swinging like a pendulum. A backup dancer for the group waved giant reproductions of their album cover like the Ten Commandments.

Onstage, Crazy A yelled "Jump! Jump!" in his mediocre English as the House of Pain imitation continued. "Jump! Jump! Jump!" he yelled.

"Busy Bee is in the house!" he continued, knowing goddamn well that the Old School legend was not anywhere on the continent. But, hey, he had to make this audience feel he had that Black rap soul somehow, didn't he? A sunnier track began, causing A to abandon the hardcore pose and lapse into commercially viable dance rap, exactly what *Doki Doki Shichau*'s producers really wanted, easy listening, non-threatening inanity—just like back home in the good ol' U.S. of A., where *Soul Train* and *Yo! MTV Raps* were more popular than ever. All around the world the same song.

Crazy A's companions studiously attempted dance moves misappropriated from A Tribe Called Quest videos. To A's left, the Q-Tip clone in earth tones and ersatz African patterns; to his right, the "brother" with the George Hamilton tan and Ohio State hooded sweatshirt. Wack as they were, they continued glaring at Luke. Their imitation of American hardcore was perfect right down to the disdain for simpler "booty" rap, but they'd still have to perform with the tacky 2 Live Crew banner behind them.

In the green room, a replenished Luke put his glass down and decided that he'd need a CD player. Fuck the DAT. During his call-and-response routines, the mainstay of his live show, the foreigners wouldn't understand what was expected of them, would not comply with his requests that they too yell, "Pop that pussy!" He'd look wack, like he couldn't exert influence over the audience, an ability respected since hip-hop's birth.

Not understanding the significance Luke was attaching to it, the show's promoters kept saying a CD player was unnecessary. The Tei-chiku Records distribution reps viewed this as a perfect opportunity to reveal their true agenda. They knew that Luke was having problems with the original 2 Live Crew, that he was overseas to promote a new solo album; but they wanted him to pretend that this ragtag band of dancers were actually the better-known 2 Live Crew. Who would know the difference? Besides, the Japanese were more familiar with the 2 Live's tried-and-true music. They wanted to hear "Me So Horny" and other famous pop hits! "As I told you this show is not

Gangsta: Merchandising the Rhymes of Violence

only for people who like rap," Itomi told a distressed Luke. "It is for people who like all music!" Luke could have told them that all of the music sounds the same, that the 2 Live Crew's records were no different or better than his current work, but he didn't. He seemed to realize that he was being tied to a past he wished to abandon.

A minute later, pensive and vexed, he sat on a couch, staring at a wall while his manager Michael Hopkins negotiated with the tensed label reps. The editor of *Crap Sheet* sighted an opportunity to distinguish his paper from *The Source* and ran to interview Crazy A in their dressing room, while the lead rhymer was receiving a haircut. After sliding past Hopkins and label reps, two Asian groupies crept into the greenroom: one of them, a dark-toned Mariah Carey clone in a tight mini was dubbed "Big Mama" by Luke, who was so cheered up by the large ass he could not overcome the size of. He began to tease her, rubbing his hand on her skirt, urging her to remove her clothing.

A female dancer joined in, running sharp fingernails down Big Mama's quivering thighs. "She don't wanna do it," the dancer mocked. Everyone's eyes were glazed with liquor and lust; the room fit the right-wing Moral Majority definition of immorality. It was like a den of pagans. The fat-assed Asian groupie was surrounded by leering Black faces. Wicked women rubbed her body, Luke lightly tugged on her waistline, letting her know she should now remove her skirt.

Big Mama held a Dixiecup filled with Bacardi, thrilled to be the center of attention. "Hey? You shy?" Luke cooed, pointing her towards me. "He's a journalist from a major feature magazine. Show him your outfit!" She smiled, surrounded by warm Black people, feeling truly accepted. Why, she'd even tanned her skin to look like them!

Her hands lifted the hem of her skirt, revealing zebra-striped panties that were wedged in the middle of her large, glowing heart-shaped ass — one of the largest I'd ever seen.

I gulped, smiled politely and may have even bowed as I'd seen Toshiro Mifune do in karate movies, and watched silently as that plump, angelic ass swung towards the exit. She had freaked out. Someone may have grabbed her vagina. "See you on Monday," said Luke, alluding to an upcoming show. Brushing past the empty, crumpled McDonald's wrappers that littered the table, his hand grabbed for the drained fifth of Bacardi. The female dancers were now in their skimpiest outfits — really nothing more than strings with tiny patches of cloth to cover nipples and their [censored]s—and practiced gyrating and twisting their hips and rears. Typical strip-club moves seen in any Too $hort video. Luke had seen it all before. He turned to Ron May and discussed Big Mama's overall thickness.

The filming began. Japanese performers mixed with teenyboppers. Their costumes were absurd: genies, women in loud pink minis, an effeminate sumo in a grass hula skirt rubbing his bloated gut with both hands—all swaying to an annoying, piped-in techno groove. Tightly edited rock samples and sound effects mixed with whiny voices and stentorian booms: the sound-effects men had stolen everything!

A thin Aladdin clone raised a large pink ceramic whale over his head with both arms, shaking it like a maraca. Then two Japanese men came out. I thought they were coal miners, until I saw that they were wearing blackface. Luke saw them in their maroon Hammer-like tuxedos and glowered. Shook his head. To him, the Japanese had fulfilled an evil prophecy: "I don't like that shit. That's like the old 'Charlie Chaplin' days, But fuck it. Watch this. Just for that I'm'a dis their hoes!"

The blackface twins—"Brother Tom" and "Brother Coon"—were a cherished act who appeared on the show every week. For sideline money they appeared in nightclubs.

Disapproving, Luke walked away from them. The hosts of the show surfaced from backstage. One of them wore a porkpie hat modeled after Fab 5 Freddy, oversized shades and a fake "African" necklace. The other had a purple mohawk, two-piece tux and Reeboks.

The camera swung to a more dynamic angle and the hosts motioned for Luke to approach. "Luke! Basketball! Basketball!" Fake Fab yelled, emphasizing that "basketball" was a slang term for Black sex, meaning Luke lived for it—reinforcing the worldwide stereotype that all Blacks, with the exception of Michael Jackson and MC Hammer, are only good for sports or pornographic action. Visibly drunk, Luke went along with it. Anything to sell records. "Yeah," he slurred at a stageful of curvy women in bikinis. "Who wants to play basketball with me?"

He looked down at the bikini-clad beauty on the table of fruit. The hosts said Luke could have his way with her. He lodged a banana between her hefty breasts and chewed it, lips touching the nervous girl's

Gangsta: Merchandising the Rhymes of Violence

cleavage, then contorted his back and began pumping his crotch toward her face.

Then Luke was led towards a stage, to judge a beauty contest. Three rows of buxom Japanese women spun for him, bent over and wiggled their chests. The winner, no surprise, was Big Mama. As the hosts tried to pull Luke away from hugging on her, he ignored them, and roamed among the contestants, using both hands to bend them over, arranging a line of them with their rears extended and slapping their asses like bongos. He even lifted one and pumped his crotch at her vagina, airborne style.

The next afternoon, the crew waited in the hotel lobby. Luke emerged from an elevator in sunglasses and a *Wanna Rock* T-shirt (the title of the solo album he was trying to promote). As we piled into a cab that resembled a squad car, everyone noticed that Luke was trying to ignore Sawako Matsuo, the tiny young hatchet-faced promoter for Teichiku Records. Sawako was rushing around, barking orders and intent on shuffling the group through scheduled appearances as quickly as possible. She ordered Luke into a certain car but he grabbed his crotch and warned, "I'm gonna ride you!"

We rode through bustling Tokyo streets, passing a Tower Records, a McDonald's shaped like a pagoda, a Kentucky Fried Chicken that sold franks and a spiked building that resembled an armored Gothic cathedral straight out of Anton Furst's most troubled nightmares. Itomi downplayed the blackface twins. "The generation now thinks Black people look good, look cool. The generation years ago, they were being sarcastic about Blacks and they don't really understand the hip-hop thing, so when this TV station usually puts rap on TV, the older generation in their thirties or forties say rappers look stupid. They are just being sarcastic. What was seen on that show, that's very different than the way everyone is using it." The air in the cab seemed static with unanswered questions as Itomi, a smidge embarrassed, looked out the window. She was kind of cute when she wasn't condoning racism.

We pulled up to the Metropolitan Plaza, a towering shopping mall made almost entirely of glass that attracted foreign tourists with its anglicized name. As Sawako paid the various cab drivers, we stood in the middle of a rush of tourists and shoppers. They banged into each other and kept walking, crossing streets in large lines. Luke wandered over and explained his latest pseudonym, "Captain Dick, like Captain America."

Our destination was the HMV store. "Me So Horny" blared on the in-store system. A Japanese voice kept blabbing over it. "Luke 2 Live!" it kept yelling.

The makeshift greenroom was a back office where shoplifters were taken until police arrived: a tiny space where employees ate lunch, gossiped, propositioned each other, stole merchandise in bags or sipped tea. Sawako's voice grew harsher, colder and less tolerant. Reclining in a chair, Luke sipped a beverage and denounced a remix of "Wanna Rock." Teichiku were taking liberties with his music. "They like that shit better than the original?!" he yelled.

"Listen," said the ever-patient Michael Hopkins, Luke's childhood friend, now his manager, again negotiating with contumacious Teichiku reps. "He doesn't like that version—"

"That is the only one we have," Sawako answered.

"You don't have the original?" Michael asked again, grabbing his forehead at the sight of the Japanese huddling together.

In the store, a small press table was set up on a tiny stage. The gray room was filled with racks of records, vintage funk and soul CDs, posters for American rock groups and the sounds of the Poison Clan, a group on Luke's label, a song dissing Dr. Dre and Compton. There were long lines surrounding the stage area. Customers had purchased Luke or 2 Live Crew albums and wanted them autographed.

His second album would be about "Japanese sex 'cause I got to experience it," Luke joked. Congenial bullshit like this helped sell albums. Give each city its props and they'd pay your mortgage.

Seated at Luke's side like a queen at a jousting tournament, Itomi fielded questions from an HMV hostess. "They want to know about Ice-T's 'Cop Killer,'" she told Luke, who sat up, adjusted his sunglasses and said: "The government doesn't want us talking about how cops kill Black youth every day in America." A young Japanese boy tilted the brim of his white *40 Acres and a Mule* hat, brushing aside the large price tag still attached to it. "Right-wing organizations made up of rich white folks have a problem with kids associating with Black folks. Anything that tells the truth about racism or housing? These rich white folks don't wanna hear about it! I mainly talk about sex and they don't wanna hear about how big a Black man's thing is!" Itomi nod-

Gangsta: Merchandising the Rhymes of Violence

ded grimly. "They would like to know your feelings on Japanese rap," she said.

"The one I heard last night sounds good. I been listening to Japanese rap for a coupl'a years. The one from last night was good but I didn't understand what he was saying."

A b-boy in an X-Tra Large lumberjack coat, khakis and dancing shoes stepped closer. Ron May kept his eyes on him. Who knew where the next Mark David Chapman would be? The b-boy's jacket flipped open, exposing nothing but a heavy-metal T-shirt—all skulls, screaming eagles and silver. "My plans while I'm here? We gonna try to hit some clubs tonight, try to pick up some girls. . . ." I scanned the audience and saw many Cypress Hill goatees, Raiders jackets, hooded sweatshirts and bandannas. Doc Martens were the British influence on the Compton look.

The next stop was Tower Records, HMV's biggest competitor. A Japanese kid with a driven facial expression and samurai ponytail entered the room. Two heavily tanned, made-up females hung on his arms. If he hadn't been wearing his disco Mix Club jacket, people would've thought he was a babyfaced pimp. DJ Toshi, Sawako informed us all, was "champion DJ in Japan!" After shaking hands— "How do you do?" "Pleased to meet you"—Luke and the crew focused on his dancers.

"Hey!"

"How are you!"

Locking one in a bear hug that would distract from hands brushing against her tits and ass, Mike Fresh complimented their Ewing jackets, models not available in the states yet. Afterwards he returned to his drink. Still grouchy, Sawako rushed to Mike and said he'd better order food now if he wanted to eat. Food could not be brought into the performance area. "What you want?" she barked. "Kentucky," Luke answered, facing her for a second then watching some of the nightly fifth pour into his glass. Last night, he said while sipping, he fucked one girl while the "contest winner," Big Mama, waited outside of his door until seven A.M. He sat back, sipping from his drink again. "Who would'a thought that rap would make it in Japan?"

Outside, the skies began to darken. Out of a window, you could see the train station below, crowded to capacity, and how the term *rush hour* assumed a whole new meaning over here. A sea of corporate types crushed against themselves. It was like the Super Bowl getting to where you were going.

Sawako kept bitching—telling him to behave in Tower—and Luke put down his Hennessy (the Bacardi was long gone). "Look!" he yelled at Itomi. "You tell Sawako that she's dealing with motherfuckers that run record companies and understand the importance of record stores! Tell her to stop fucking talking to us like we children!" After Itomi translated, in a quick whir of words, Sawako, humbled and offended, rushed off.

Walking through the store, Luke spotted Tomo, the Teichiku rep with the Peter Frampton hair. "Hey! Tomo the homo!" he laughed, before sipping his drink. Tomo didn't find this amusing but concealed his anger. Even smiled. Upstairs in a closet-size room, Luke reclined in a seat as readers of a Japanese music fanzine posed questions. "Your name is Minekko?" he asked, intrigued by an overdeveloped teenage girl with a baby face.

Fan: "Do you go to nightclubs?"

Luke: "Yeah, I have to 'cause if I don't, I'll lose touch with the people."

"If you weren't a performer, what would you be doing?"

"I'd be a jacker. I can't kiss nobody's ass. I don't think I could work for anybody else. I'm one of the most notorious felons."

"Do you like men?"

"No! No! No! No men! Just women! [To me:] That's a new one, shit!"

"Who was your biggest influence?"

"Malcolm X." [Suggesting that he was more political than any of his dance-floor fiends would ever imagine.]

"Can you tell us what is so great about Malcolm X? We are Japanese, we only see the surface."

"He was a great Black man. Some of the things he went through, he told us we would still be through today. He brought a lot of awareness to what's still happening in the United States." [Luke mugged for the Japanese photographer].

"What are you doing for Christmas?"

"I'm'a hang with my three little daughters."

"Daughters?" [They can't understand. This is Luke. Black man Luke. Basketball sex.]

"Maybe open some Christmas presents . . ."

"How do you raise your daughters?"

"I raise them the way my mama raised me! [While the young girls wished to hear of his sexploits, he instead launched into advice.] Don't just watch TV and think all Black people — all Americans — are bad. . . ." [The message was translated and the girls smiled.]

"If you were reincarnated, would you want to come back as a man or a woman?"

"What?! This the same one that asked that other question?! I'd like to come back as man because I like this piece of meat I have between my legs! [Before Itomi translated, Luke faced her.] Naw, don't say that. [Itomi agreed, since these were "virginal young girls still in high school," causing Luke to ramble on about the ratio of men to women on the planet, citing various statistics until he brought things right back to his "piece of meat."] I wouldn't trade it for anything in the world!!!"

During his in-store performance, Luke, Japan's newest sex god, oversaw a circus of flesh. Businessmen sang along. They shoved against the barricades. "Shake that pussy," they yelled, mad with lust and more than ready to loosen their ties. In strategically torn blue jeans and skimpy black tops, the Black women did their seductive Alvin Ailey moves. Luke paced back and forth, offering them to the public, knowing damn well he wouldn't let it go down between his girls and the rubes.

Two Latino kids in heavy leather coats approached me. The bald-headed one said, "We're from New York." His partner, a kid with a samurai topknot and what looked like a penciled-on mustache, handed me a demo. "Over there, they got all these rap groups so I came over here with my dancers cause there ain't no competition! I thought it would be easier," said MegaFlash. He'd be returning to America, a failure, in a few weeks, he admitted.

A short Japanese girl with big tits walked by, speaking English. Mega grabbed her hand, stopped her and spoke softly with lips near her ear. Unimpressed, she rolled her eyes. Then she looked my way and frowned. "Fuck you," I told her. A minute later, her finger tapped my shoulder.

"Sorry," I said: the usual I'm-under-so-much-stress shit. She apologized as well. She thought I was like the other Americans she had encountered at hip-hop shows. Just another American storming through Japan like a conqueror, claiming women and treating everyone like hired help.

"I'm smarter than I look," I said.

"You do not look so bad," she answered.

After the show, in front of the store, surrounded by a sea of neon, I told Luke I'd ride back to the Hotel Creston in my new friend's car. "*Source*-man's gonna get some ass!" he yelled. "Yo, be careful," advised Ron May.

We walked back to her black Suzuki Alto, me feeling ten feet tall.

"You like jazz?" Emiko asked, driving past beautiful parks. "It's bad! Watch."

A delicate hand pressed PLAY on her car radio. Out came A Tribe Called Quest's *Low End Theory*. Her smile was pleasant. She moved her shoulder as she drove. I was happy sitting next to her, comforted by her presence thousands of miles from New York. Underneath the Nike Ewing jacket, soft full young breasts. Her ass was pronounced in tight biker shorts. Her high-top black leather Filas added the necessary sangfroid.

If I slept with her, it would be like fucking an exotic girl from the East Village, someone visiting the country who wanted to experience as much of America as she could. It would be a good morning: cigarettes, hugs, life stories and vows of love.

"It's illegal to have a speaker-box" she said, ending the silence. "If we see a police I have to turn it down. It's loud for a lot of people who live around here, but when I see them I turn it down. If I listen loud to this, cops check my speakers and say, 'Please lower this.'" As the melancholic grooves of "Butter" faded—the song always left me blue—she said she really loved jazz music, that she really wanted to sing on records, that she had been a hip-hop fan for two years; that, prior to that, she had followed the New Kids on the Block. "Can you believe it?" she smiled, all grown up.

Emiko told me that listening to rap fueled her desire to learn Eng-

Gangsta: Merchandising the Rhymes of Violence

lish, that R&B's Mary J. Blige was a surrogate teacher. "I feel bad because I feel I don't have the talent like this Black people," she said as she raised the volume. "They got real talent in everything—in voice, talent, in music . . . They don't try to be that. I'm proud to be Japanese but I want to be different than other Japanese artists. They all do the same thing. If I do something different, they'll see that quickly." She wanted to make music "for the States."

At a red light on an empty road near a municipal building of some sort, she quickly switched her radio off. Four policemen were running towards her car. Instead they harassed four Arab men on the sidewalk behind us. "Oh, they're Arab," she noticed. "Fuck the Irans!"

She pulled off and I turned to watch the policemen separate the startled drunks from each other. The cops scowled; the drunks were ecstatic; their fists clenched. All around the world the same song.

She parked in what appeared to be an alley behind the hotel, listening to my demo as I killed another can of Asahi. The street was dark with small buildings and towering thick-barred fences. A door opened across the street; a squat Japanese man shuffled towards us in robe and sandals. He tapped on the window and began shouting at Emiko. She lowered the volume on "Run Devil Run." He scuffled home and she shrugged. "He lives there. The music is very loud. He said if he must come out again he will bring a gun." She stopped me from following him. The police would throw me in jail, she reminded.

We walked up to my room. I offered drinks and, to make peace, even invited *Crap Sheet* over for a beer. Emiko said she had a boyfriend in New York. She spoke of how women bowed and scraped and let men run the show over here. "That's why I always get American boyfriend. I don't like the Japanese way!" I could already imagine her under me, squirming as I thrust my dick in her. My heart soared as I finished two cans of Asahi and tried to convince her to stay a bit longer. She spoke English and she seemed cool, and I was lonely for company. I didn't want to be left alone with a fridgeful of beer and whiskey, thinking about my brother Jay's suicide three weeks ago in the South Bronx. "I can't," she said.

Tomorrow was a school day at her university and her mother would miss her if she spent the night out. I opened up a small bottle of whiskey and swigged it back before asking if I could then see her tomorrow. "Tomorrow I go see Hammer!" she said. And nothing would interfere with those plans. Hammer was like a deity over here: Hammer, Michael Jackson, Bobby Brown and now Luke.

November 16, 1992: I was summoned to Luke's suite at noon. One of the largest on the premises, it was filled with tables, a huge television set, plush carpeting and a truly well-stocked liquor cabinet. Kiyomi Matsunaga from *Pump* magazine was asking Itomi questions. What kind of kid were you? Luke's answer was brief and vague. "In Japan, it's hard for us to imagine what kind of trouble you would get in," Itomi said, wanting him to elaborate, to give this interviewer the Black Caesar story she wanted. "Were you ever in any trouble?"

Luke flashed a knowing smile, one that said, *Oh, I get it.*

"Oh yeah," he answered, "I been in my fair share with guns and shoot-outs. You don't think about it when you do it, you just do it."

"Did you feel you had the knowledge to be a businessman? Some people don't feel they do."

"Just growing up in the streets is 'business' in terms of making money," he said, a bit annoyed by the "some people" part. "Street life is like college. That's why a lot of us call it 'sidewalk university.' " He segued into his golden rule: Don't fuck people over because it is a small world; avoid getting a bad reputation because it will stick with you. "You have to respect the people you're dealing with," he said, fixing Kiyomi with a dead stare.

"And so you went into music business? Why music?"

He started at local high schools, he explained, before moving his parties to white-owned skating rinks. Rink owners let him hold "Soul Nights" and Luke booked Run-DMC. His clientele grew, and one guy asked Luke to help him record an ode to the events. "But they didn't pay us, so we figured, if we could make them dance with one record, we'll do another."

"Were the Soul Nights for white people or Black people only?"

"It was a white skating rink but it was for Black people," he stressed, not wanting to be depicted as another Michael Jackson or Lionel Ritchie. "It was ninety-eight percent Black on that night of the week."

Kiyomi's next question was about Malcolm X. "She has heard the wrong information, that he would start violence," Itomi explained.

Luke sighed, clarified, then said, "I'm really interested in seeing

Gangsta: Merchandising the Rhymes of Violence

the movie. I personally feel they're gonna make it watered-down, to portray him as someone he really ain't."

Kiyomi Matsunaga felt her question on Malcolm had opened Pandora's box, her interview would be too political, so she shifted gears — she wanted to discuss something sensational, like his "controversial" live shows. "Some people are thinking, 'Why doesn't he get arrested?'" The United States government was behind the media's negative opinion of him, Luke explained. But how come Madonna could get onstage with her "ass hanging out" — pretending to fuck dancers — and escape the harassment he was suffering? He didn't know. "When I do something similar to what she's doing, they want to arrest me!" Still, he vowed to never change. "If you're a man, you're a man, and if you're a mouse, you're a mouse. I'll go down being a man, fighting for what I believe in."

He thumbed through an issue of *The Source*, with Spike Lee and Charles Barkley on the cover. "I do mostly chants, call-and-response. The crowd plays a big part. The 2 Live Crew do more rapping about sexual things."

"What do you feel people should never do?"

"You should never be involved in any way with kiddie porn. You have a lot of wild-ass people that get off on abusing kids." Matsunaga asked if Luke was a father. "You fuck with my kids and you're dead!" he roared. A shaken Matsunaga thanked him for the interview and meekly requested an autograph. "Sure, sure, no problem," he said, friendly smiles again.

After the *Pump* photo shoot, Luke left the hotel. Itomi crossed the lobby and plopped down on the couch. She was exhausted. "To tell you the truth, the hip-hop scene is dying out here. A lot of people got into it just for the fashion. Did you go to Julianna's last night? It's the only real disco we have over here. We used to have more but now they're closing them down to make way for Karaoke houses."

At nightfall, Luke emerged from the elevator and crossed the spacious lobby as imperiously as Darth Vader striding through the corridors of the Death Star. "They say the first show's gonna be ehh, but the second show's gonna have more people," he told the dancers. "What the fuck y'all looking at? Let's go!" Most of Luke's audience would be attending the Hammer concert. Skies were dark. Crowded van. Dancers talking shit. From outside, the On-Air Club looked like a slaughterhouse, covered with sheets of steel. Inside, it was like being in any New York hip-hop club: cold blue light, sticky dance floor, brightly lit bars, kids who liked hip-hop. In his dressing room, Luke relaxed with a bottle and Kentucky Fried Chicken; in the background a techno remix of A Tribe Called Quest's "Can I Kick It." The club's promoter, Soichiro "Sony" Kimura of F.B.I. Japan Inc.—clad in a black suit like the villains in cheesy action films—rushed up. "You no make show too naked!" he yelled. His hair stood up. He waved an angry finger like a sword. "They call the police! Police close the show!"

On the stage, DJ Toshi scratched "Good Times," manipulating Chic's bass line until it sounded like dancehall reggae. Wannabe roughnecks sat on the floor with their backs against walls, resting hands on upraised knees. Toshi's dancers, the heavily tanned beauties, ran out in g-strings and gyrated stiffly, their mimicry a tribute to the Black women referred to as "sisters" by Japanese b-boys. I wondered if Sir Mix-A-Lot knew they were using "Baby Got Back" for strip routines out here.

A bit of a show-off, Toshi displayed an array of tricks. Like Flash in his prime, he spun around, used elbows, feet, anything to scratch the record. In Disco Mix Club battles, he made opponents worldwide groan in defeat. That night, he used records by Public Enemy and Run-DMC to remind us of his achievements. "Number one!" Chuck's debut single yelled, followed by DMC (on the "Jam Master Jay" single) saying his name. The audience stopped dancing and faced this maniac onstage. All they heard was "Number one / DMC / Number one / DMC." Next he took Everlast's voice from House of Pain's "Jump Around"—"JumpJumpJumpJump" the turntable screeched. Calculating as ever, he played "Baby Got Back" again and out came the Bobsy twins with their asses and hair weaves. Little babies in the crowd—half Black, half Japanese—danced near their parents.

When Luke hit the stage, everyone cheered. "How many ladies like sucking dick?!" he wailed. Female dancers ran out as beats boomed. A few English hecklers—servicemen from a nearby U.S. Army base—hushed up when Luke started chanting. They couldn't front: his music made people feel good, and they knew that Luke inadvertently

Gangsta: Merchandising the Rhymes of Violence

defended the civil liberties and Constitutional rights of all Americans. His battle against Blowhard County censors had become a National Issue.

Myth had it that the Japanese were calm and meditative. The men at this concert were anything but. They yelled, roared, howled or whistled. Called onstage to dance with the ladies, they pawed asses and did their best to try fucking them. After the first dance routine, Luke reemerged from behind the curtain. His Bacardi consumed, he yelled, "We gonna have group sex in this motherfucker!" The crowd exploded. The ladies continued shaking. "We need a fucking interpreter up here! How the fuck you say 'sucking pussy' in Japan?! Bank-O? All right! Mo-Bank-O, Mo-Bank-O, Mo-Bank-O!"

Three lucky nerds onstage had their faces sat on. The girls simulated fucking them in chairs, rubbing those soft, warm tits against them and placing their hands on their asses and hips. One nerd went too far during a 69 with Desire. The pervert dug his tongue between her thick legs, trying to move her g-string aside and enter. Luke stood over them, frowning, and yelled, "Bank-O!" Backstage, the club's promoter Sony adjusted his jacket, ran a hand through his slicked-back black hair and interrupted our conversation. Ordered me from my seat, and I refused. Ron May called me over. Sony was behind him. "He's the promoter and he feels you offended him!" Sony's face was puffed up and tomato red. He threatened to have me on the next plane back to New York.

"Do what you have to do," I said.

Sony yelled that he would. "You just obey me!" he screamed.

I told him to go fuck himself.

"Don't worry about Sony," Luke said a minute later. "He fucking with you? You with me! Hey, Ron May! You tell Sony not to be fucking with these reporters! They with me! You tell him he's worrying about the wrong thing again!" Luke returned to his Bacardi and Coke, and to the three groupies in the room. The Black woman Luke had flown in from Chicago, whom *Crap Sheet* had tried to pick up all day, fumed.

By now, I was trashed—four cans of Kirin in my hotel room, one-hour nap, ride to the club, four or five Bacardi and Cokes. The evening ended with Luke taking the Chicagoan back to his room, *Crap Sheet* feeling like the horse's ass and me drinking in my room with a crowded mind.

The next afternoon, DJ Mike Fresh and I explored the side streets of Tokyo, where houses and roads were smaller, walls were filthy and the air reeked of gutted fish. We walked in the road as sidewalks were blocked by garbage bags from small shops. Fresh was away from Tokyo's crowded streets and the sex-obsessed road crew. He bopped down the street, projecting the image of a take-no-shit Black American. "You can get killed just for talking if someone hears and doesn't like what you're saying," he said of Miami. Unemployment was high; people dealt drugs; automatic weaponry was easy to come by; and Superfly wannabes were misogynist. "Hoes don't wanna do nothing for themselves! They just want a nigga to buy them things. A lot are coming from Atlanta to work in the strip clubs. A lot of college girls figure, 'Fuck it, I could make all this money faster if I dance!'

"They just doing what they gotta do, and everybody gets mad at Luke 'cause of what he be saying, but there are women like those he talks about—hoes that just don't wanna do nothing but come-up. You'll see them after the shows, just waiting there for him to finish up with some other bitch. They don't respect themselves; they just wanna be with him 'cause they think it's a 'prestige' thing, like that girl from Chicago. He's with all these other girls and she don't say nothing. Maybe she don't give a fuck; maybe she just wanna be seen with Luke. That's why niggas don't care in Miami. A lot of the girls are like that so niggas see them and right away say, 'Yo, ho, what's up! You wanna fuck?!' If you come up with intelligence, these hoes'll wanna sucker you."

The second night at the On-Air Club and Sony Soichiro was as calm as the earth tones of his suit. He was acting milder, benign, his voice gentler as he stood near me on the balcony. By choice, I was avoiding the dressing room; too many bottles of liquor, too much KFC.

The club was bathed in hot scarlet light, and more crowded: people wore hoodies, Carhart gear, wool scully caps, military fatigues, three-quarter-length leather jackets and three-piece suits. Yuppies eager for nudity besieged the bartender with cries for Kirin or Asahi; kids in Raiders gear swaggered around, living in their own private Comptons. They considered it a form of flattery, this hip-hop re-creation, an escape from the mundanity of everyday life in a country where individuality was frowned upon. The hip-hop gear was their costume, like the jail suits many West Coast rappers wore to convey their hardness.

Three Black men walked in with American Flag dewrags. Their cowboy boots and ankle jeans ruined the desired effect, which was to look tough, Black and dangerous.

On-Air was a decent if somewhat soulless re-creation of the over-hyped and equally plastic American subculture. The stage area was impenetrably dark; only the blood-red eyes of two turntables — one for Toshi, one for Mike Fresh — were visible. A dark-skinned Japanese girl leaned over the balcony, providing me with a lovely view of her cleavage. I was becoming a pervert. Her lips were coated with crimson lipstick, gold doorknocker earrings hung from her lobes, her hair piled atop her head in the "babydoll" fashion popularized in LL Cool J videos. She was twenty, a salesgirl in a department store by day, convincing yuppies to buy more business attire. By night, she immersed herself in the music, fashion and culture of another race. All the while she yearned for an identity of her own.

"Last summer, I was in the sun," she began. "My hair long and curly. No gold" — she flicked a necklace for emphasis — "but yes, silver. I wanted to be a 'sister' because they are cool and beautiful and soulful. I saw movie: you know *Rage in Harlem*? The woman, 'Sister,' is very, very cool and beautiful." She hadn't wanted to be like the thin subservient women most Japanese men preferred so she adopted a tougher persona, enlarged her lips and bosom, grew her hair long, curled it and tanned her complexion. "I wanted to get away from Japanese culture but my friends and parents say to me, 'You are not good girl!' " She was now a "sister."

"To be a 'sister,' you listen to rap, you be tough, drink a lot, drive a car and have fun! I think we able to be like a 'brother' or 'sister' easy. We can sometimes make like a 'sister's hair, curly hair, but we cannot be able to be white people so . . . We can much better be like Japanese."

"Why are you trying to look like Black people?"

"Because we cannot have blue eyes. We can be Black but not white. I feel everybody is same in Japan. They don't try to do different thing. I don't like that. It is not cool to be same so I want to do something different. I want to do something when I want to do it. They don't like trouble so they stay the same. To be at the top is very hard position. Everyone see you up there and they watch what you do. Is easier to hide."

The dressing-room door opened and she saw Luke. She tossed her cigarette to the floor. "I go now, okay?"

Interracial couples were everywhere: Jordan-scaled suit-clad Black men hugged Yoko-like women, unaware that they were pawns in a national game of "Let's make Daddy angry!"

Then Luke came out again, totally blasted, intent on stirring things up before leaving for Osaka in the morning. "I need a girl who wants to have sex with me!" he almost pleaded. Mike Fresh threw on a beat and the "real" Luke was back, selecting three women from the crowd for his male dancers. The R&B ballad was replaced by a faster beat: Luke signaled his female dancers and out they came! They ripped off their tops and panties and wiggled their asses at the audience. Desire wasn't wearing a thing below her bellybutton. Another dancer jiggled tiny boobs with both hands. The women from the audience were led offstage, but Emiko sat there. Luke muttered into the microphone. "I'm gonna make this bitch suck my dick," he smirked. He assumed that Emiko didn't understand English and fumbled with his belt buckle. Words could not describe the look of total horror on Luke's face when she leaped up and yelled, "No! I'm not doing that!"

"Why'd you think I let you stay on the stage? C'mon, relax!"

"I'm not doing that!" she shrieked, running even as Luke blocked her path.

"Then get your crabby ho ass off the stage!" he shouted. As he led the crowd in a chant of "Fuck that ho!" she bolted offstage and ran for the balcony. I saw her coming and, not wanting to lose sight of her, yelled, "Stay right there! Don't move!"

"Emiko! How could you?!" I asked, standing across from her in a stairway.

"I didn't know!" So fucked up at times, this life I live. Everybody tells me I'm a good writer. I don't really feel that.

102

Gangsta: Merchandising the Rhymes of Violence

I caught myself. "I'm sorry! I'm going to miss you. Damn!"

"I'm sorry, Ronin. I did not mean for this to happen." She wasn't talking about the Luke show.

"I know. Damn . . . Stay with me, Emiko." Alcohol had fucked me up.

"Ronin," she said, watery eyes, "I feel so bad, I—"

"Listen! Fuck those people! You were right not to do that! Fuck them! Why are you sad? 'Cause you didn't suck Luke's dick?! Come with me, we'll talk."

"Ronin, I'm sorry. I can't. If I stay, I will miss you more when you leave. Please let me go."

Everything hit me at once and I was numb . . . hating life. "Okay. Okay but . . ."

"Ronin, please," she said, water streaming from the corner of an eye. I wanted to console her after what happened onstage. She stared at her feet, told herself "They hate me. I ruined the show. I should have . . ."

It was one of the hardest things I'd ever had to do, but I turned and walked away without saying good-bye. To this day, it still fucks me up; the fact that I had so many so-called "friends" in the states who are really full of shit when it comes down to it—each with their own little motive.

This was the final night in Tokyo. Crushed between dancers in a cab. Tomorrow this circus—and *Crap Sheet*, the biggest "Ro" clone ever—would head to Osaka, where they'd chant profanity, strip, drink and romp with groupies. Luke had to get drunk to do the things he did.

Some of MC Hammer's dancers and road crew hooked up with Luke's crew. Julianna's was a large, noisy and pretentious club: a trendy disco where snooty waiters served corporate alcoholics. Everyone drank a little. Trendy assholes, snobby waiters, hookers out for fame, a society that simultaneously admired and hated these musicians—it was all too much. I felt lost in Japan, land of the fake hip-hop fans and redneck wannabe Blacks. Sex sex sex, lust, dancing, stripping call-and-response . . . too much. I wanted to leave immediately. My heart was broken, my faith in humanity diminished. Big Mama rolled up at Julianna's.

Crap Sheet and a Hammer dancer said some stupid comment, and we almost came to blows. Luke leaned against a bar, ignoring the woman from Chicago. She had drunk one too many and was now dead on her feet. I suggested he get her some water, then said I'd be leaving tomorrow. Nursing a drink, slightly disappointed, he said, "Fine. Whatever you want."

It was four A.M. in my hotel room. The third and last can of post-Bacardi beer was finished. Outside, the streets were empty. The ashtray was filled to capacity. Images of Emiko onstage and Luke ordering her off, and the audience cursing her, filled my mind. I called my soon-to-be-ex in America and talked with her about this, about hanging with Emiko in my room and discussing her life in Japan, about a land where Japanese women are tired of being subservient. Why her on that stage? The whole crowd booing her. Why?

Chapter 7

Life After Death

Zev Love X was dressed in that shade of black worn by mourners. In low spirits, he filled the dim-lit conference room with a palpable tension. The blunt cigar he waved clouded the air with impermeable smoke and made seeing his face difficult. A bandmate in the trio sipped from an almost empty 40 of Olde English 800, the malt liquor of choice for many hip-hop drinkers. It was one in the afternoon, early to be finishing a bottle, and we were in his label's offices in the Time Warner Building, a mortuary, really, for uncompromising music.

The offices were staffed with white employees and the sounds of their newest grunge band. It was difficult to feel comfortable in the belly of the corporate hydra. Time Warner censored hip-hop records then pimped the culture in *Vibe*, their "upscale" hip-hop magazine.

Self-promotion took a backseat to thoughts of Zev's brother Subroc, the other member of KMD (Kausing Much Damage) who had been killed by a car after their new album was completed. Zev's features seemed hardened; the face not as innocent as it was three years ago. The striped shirts were gone, and the wire-frame glasses that he wore in ads for their debut of the album *Mr. Hood*. Today he dressed like a paramilitary.

"I can't fuck with all that image shit, being under somebody's coattails," he said, disavowing his past and revealing his unhappiness. Elektra had underpromoted *Mr. Hood* to ghetto audiences and marketed the group as Native Tonguers, he told me. They had fabricated an image around the more accessible cut, "Peachfuzz," and not "Nitty Gritty," which represented their worldview. "Peachfuzz" had been a puppy-love ditty; "Nitty Gritty" was a diatribe against white devils.

"I feel a lot of things changed from our original idea as opposed to now, where we got to keep all the real shit," he said. "Our first time, we didn't even know how to fuck with it: shit fucking up, everybody getting in between this creative shit—" But *Black Bastards* was a different album. It was closer to the sound they had when they were discovered by Serch, a white MC with the group 3rd Bass. "They were always talented," Serch said of discovering the duo in Long Beach, Long Island. "But I knew they were spending too much time in that room with their equipment. You should've seen it." Apparently, the room was cluttered with furniture, records and rhyme books. Long insects crawled in from their lawn outside. He was no longer involved with them, Serch said, but he hoped Zev would calm down. "He was always getting into trouble when he was younger."

Serch hoped Zev would channel his anger into new material. Inspired by Last Poet Gylan Kain's *Blue Guerrilla*, *Black Bastards* was a pointed reaction to hip-hop's current fatalism. Wavering between life affirmation and out-and-out nihilism, Zev spoke of attacking people with wine bottles ("Sweet Premium"), buying a new handgun ("Get U Now"), long-lost bitter loves ("Plumskinz"), the word *nigga* ("What a Nigga Know"), and whites who mimick Black culture. *Black Bastards* was confusing but powerful; relevant, focused, sophisticated and thankfully devoid of crossover-friendly abstraction. Listeners would have loved it if Time Warner hadn't dropped the group.

After this interview, Zev would be informed that he no longer had a deal. *Black Bastards'* cover—a stylized sketch of a gallows with a "Sambo" character dangling on a noose—had attracted the scorn of Terri Rossi, an R&B editor at *Billboard* who attacked it in print and suggested that the group and label needed "a refresher course on the entire civil rights movement. . . ."

"If it was anybody hanging there, it was Al Jolson or Ted Danson, doing that stupid shit he did," Zev would later say.

As he sat in the conference room, exhaling like a dragon, he couldn't have imagined that it would be over soon. He stoically answered questions, laughed to himself and held a tight rein on his emotions. "I wasn't even with him that day," he said of his brother's death.

Gangsta: Merchandising the Rhymes of Violence

"I don't know. I don't wanna get into details, really." It was a painful memory. The police had seen Zev drinking a beer in front of his home, and when his name came up in the computer, for an outstanding warrant from 1989, they placed him in custody.

". . . for drinking a couple of beers, trying to take me in for some bullshit. So I'm locked up for four hours and didn't see him till the next day." During the night, his brother died. "I don't know. That's how it happened really."

"How did you find out?" I asked.

"I felt it," he nodded. "I felt it definitely. I called my mom up right after that."

Numbness, shock and disbelief shaded his voice; I couldn't detect acceptance. I looked at Zev's buddy draining the 40 and suddenly remembered my older brother.

His wife had died of AIDS and left him with three children. He began to drink heavily and fall into deep monologues about the life they shared. He'd say that he didn't care about living anymore. Months later, I stood by his closed casket.

"Shit was real like that," Zev grieved. "I forgot who told me in words. I just knew."

I began to agree with the insiders who said Zev was in denial.

"He used to be able to articulate his thoughts in such a clear way," his publicist opined. "But now he's sullen, using beer and getting zooted as a crutch instead of facing things and trying to work it out."

Death had cast a shadow on him.

"I don't know," he said. "Niggas be passing away so much. The shit is crazy now. To tell you the truth, you just don't give a fuck no more. I mean: you give a fuck, you care about what goes on, but to a point where you now know that shit is real."

Having to promote, discuss and hear his brother's voice on *Black Bastards* reopened painful wounds, but ever the stoic, he refused to show weakness. He leaned forward and disguised his sadness with a forceful tone. "It seems like I'm listening to two different people, to tell you the truth. I'm not even that motherfucker from before. I don't know. Different times. What I'm doing now, creatively, is totally different. It's like 'him and me combined as one'–type shit." His voice tensed. His answer was stiff, painful.

"Are you uncomfortable discussing this?"

"Nah, I never did before," he deflected. "Does it sound like I'm stuttering or something? Ask me anything. I wanna talk."

The new album evoked images of "the exact time" his brother approached him with specific lyrics. Sub would barge into their room and, with the enthusiasm of youth, say: "Yo, check this shit! It's butter! Bust it! I'm'a flip it!"

". . . when he was doing it for me," Zev monotoned, memories swimming through his eyes like fish, "I remember that shit just like yesterday. It seems like one point in time, stuck there, can't change."

His mother was coping, he said, nodding, considering her pain. "She went through crazy shit as well. Word."

A prolonged silence spoke volumes.

"It's like this," he said. "The physical body is not us anyway." Human beings possessed souls, he believed: after physical death, souls were numinous. Mourning at a graveside marker amounted to "worshipping graven images."

During a pause, he toked on the diminishing blunt. Subroc would live on through his music and in people's loving memories but the pain was immense. He stared into his lap and shook a Newport out of a crumpled pack. "I feel like a fucking piece of bullshit," he said. "Plus, smoking cigarettes? I know this ain't me. This can't be me for real."

> *"When I'm gone, expect me back to haunt."*
> *— Subroc, "It Sounded Like A Roc"*

When someone dies, it gives rise to enough sadness to inspire the bluest paintings or jazz. You ask yourself if you were there when the dead needed you. My mother had died when I was thirteen and out of town. When I returned to New York, my older brother greeted me in the stairway. He was wearing a black suit and his red, puffy eyes revealed that he'd been crying. My sister hugged me tight, cried and said, "She died on Good Friday."

My mother's funeral signaled the end of my family. Her hair was combed back, she had too much blush on her cheeks and she never would've been caught dead in that frilly white dress. I stared at the black coffin in shock as it slowly descended into the cold and lonely

Gangsta: Merchandising the Rhymes of Violence

grave. When he wasn't sweet-talking the ladies, the pastor read psalms and prayed. Distant relatives wiped mud from their shoes and impatiently glanced at their wristwatches. Fiery sunlight ripped through the stripped branches on rotting trees.

Over a decade later, Zev Love X sat at a table in a shadowy room. Why call the album *Black Bastards?*

"I did that on purpose," he confidently answered. "Bold title, bold statement. To make a mockery of this bullshit system of censorship." There had been one song that stuck in my mind, a work called "Constipated Monkeys" that sampled "Bellybutton Window," a posthumous Jimi Hendrix release.

"Sub put that whole shit together," he said as reverently as a choirboy staring up at a crucifix. "That shit was flavor," he agreed.

What does "Garbage Day 3" represent? (It was a somber work: tenebrous bass, bloodcurdling screams, racial epithets, gunshots.)

"Whatever you hear or pick up out of that is mad short instances of big things. That just fills the whole gap of when people didn't see us or whatever." Its saddest moment arrives midsong, when a lugubrious female voice asks, "It's not the three of us anymore, is it?"

The sun moved from behind gray wintry clouds and into the window, shifting shadows and bringing Zev into the light. KMD would weather the storms and endure, he promised, "just as long as I can make records out this bitch." He waved his arms at office walls—not knowing executives planned to drop him—then optimistically revealed that a friend named Grim Reaper would join him.

"Shit evolves like that, you kno'm saying? Grim and me collaborate on a lot of joints. We're about to come out with some shit in the summertime. But that's really it. I'm just getting with him. After that, there'll be no more changes."

He would return to his home in Long Island and spend time with his two-year-old son, born during his hiatus from recording. "He's two," the proud father nodded. "Yep, bad just like me, too." His brother was dead but his son was alive. "It's mad fun being a parent: like being little all over again, getting to bug out, play all day—"

Chapter 8

The Beginning of the End

■

Dozens of Jheri-Kurled gangsta rappers hailed from Compton but I couldn't help viewing the region as NWA country. Their influence—the themes they tackled and their approach—ran through the work of groups that followed. Gangsta rap was tired and more than a little feculent but years after its release, while everyone else revered newer G-funk gangstas, I still guzzled 40s to NWA's *Straight Outta Compton.* That I'd be going to Compton to speak with MC Ren, about NWA and a new solo album (described by one editor as "Kill Whitey") had me excited. Seated on the corner of a bed, Ren wrestled with the controls of a Sega handset. The computer was beating the former athlete at basketball. I thought playing Sega and video games was for the pussies at *The Source.* Not for the "ruthless villain," the "Black nigga that they call Ren." But there he was, dressed in black as he was in countless NWA publicity shots, a look he admitted stealing from Run-DMC, manipulating his handset and watching his player dart across a court before glancing across the dimly lit, sparsely furnished shed.

His "boys," you could tell that these kids slamming dominoes on a makeshift table thought they were big shots: they cursed and talked tough, until one of their wifeys came in, to ask one player for loot. "I ain't got shit!" he yelled. But the baby needed milk. Sighing, he dug into his pocket and extracted sixty-five cents.

Outside, on a couch near a wooden fence, away from the profanation, Ren admitted that his friendship with Eric "Eazy-E" Wright had seen better days. They were as sociable towards each other as Christians and lions in Ancient Rome. "He stayed right around the corner but he was older," Ren (born Lorenzo Patterson) began. "He was with my brother. I got a older brother that's about twenty-eight." Discovering that young "Master Ren" actually made demos, Eric promised to release his work as a soloist—right after he completed his current projects. "But it was taking too long so he just pulled me into the group and I went from there."

Ren knew of Andre "Dr. Dre" Young from the World Class Wreckin' Cru, and from mix tapes aired on local station KDAY. Dre had introduced Ren to O'Shea "Ice Cube" Jackson, who came from another part of town and was always the comedian in NWA. In this story—as dramatic as those of the Supremes or Temptations—Cube was the hero. One afternoon back then, Ren sat with Cube in his car, waiting for Eric to get home, so they could work on music in his mother's garage. Ren popped in a recent gift, a cassette he bumped while driving. "Man, there's this tape out," he said, complimenting the lyricist. "It's tight as hell," he said, just as Cube sat up.

"That's me!" he yelled.

"Really?"

They sat in the car listening and laughing, Ren said. A variety of emotions flashed across his face as he remembered that halcyon period. In that garage with Dre and Eazy near the drum machines and samplers. Trying to stay warm on cold evenings with a tiny portable heater, 'cause "it used to be cold as shit at night."

■■

NWA had already recorded "Dope Man" and "8-Ball" for Macola Records, a nowhere label specializing in *ranchera* music, and were set to take their cover photo. An assortment of gangstas stood in an alley, wearing Adidas gear, curls and gold chains, drinking 40s and glaring at the camera with dead eyes. "I was on the album [cover] but half of my face was cut off by the NWA logo," Ren's DJ Train laughed. "It showed half of it. They put the logo on me." The same happened to Sir Jinx, a friend who would later produce Ice Cube's solo work. "Cut off with the letters too."

At Dre and DJ Yella's apartment on Paramount, the group developed their material. Cube always had a notebook, and always suggested routines for their breaks. The D.O.C. had arrived from Dallas, Texas—after Dre stole him from the Fila Fresh Crew—and the group spent entire days in the studio. Ren remembered these days as sadly as Miss Haversham did her wedding day. Doc helped Eazy-E with lyrics; Dre created beats; Ren and Cube sat in separate corners, filling notebooks.

"I kind'a miss that 'cause we used to be in there all day. All of us together. It's hard to kind'a remember some of this. That's when we were young. Not like we all 'old' but that *was* five or six years ago." Relating anecdotes from the good old days was like reliving them.

One time Dre told Cube to lay his vocals on "Parental Discretion Is Advised."

"Dre kept the beat playing over and over." Cube went first; then the group. "Doc wrote Eric's part so all the parts were tight," Ren pointed out, confirming Eazy's legendary lack of skill. The session ended but Cube, a perfectionist, said, "Fuck that!"—rushed home, rewrote his verse. Next morning, the group arrived, surprised to find Cube already there, relaxed, ready to move on to the next song, not bullshitting or raising a stink. They heard his new, stronger verse when they pressed PLAY.

As Ren spoke, I couldn't help but think about EPMD or Public Enemy and the Bomb Squad, separations that hurt all involved. NWA members had solo albums but they weren't the same. Ren seemed to have his fingers crossed, hoping that *Shock of the Hour* would at least go platinum, wishing that the future weren't so uncertain. Each of Cube's albums went platinum, and his film career was better than ever—rave reviews for *Boyz N the Hood* and a leading role in *Trespass* proved that. Dre's Death Row stable—Snoop, Rage, Korrupt, Daz and Nate Dogg—were outselling most of hip-hop and spawning dozens of imitators.

Understandably, Ren was nervous. After denouncing Black nationalism with NWA (saying, on one record: "I'm not with that 'Black' shit so I'm not gonna yell that!")—here he was with *Shock of the Hour*, a foray into more socially conscious, nationalistic themes. Musically, a slew of untested producers reworked beats Dre had provided in NWA, but their attempts at malevolent G-funk were heavy-handed and invidious.

The Beginning of the End

This wasn't the solo album envisioned many years ago, when he told Eazy he'd help with NWA, then record his own music with Train, but saw he'd have to wait, since Dre had discovered J.J. Fad and already leaped into working with them.

■■■

Now that he'd abandoned the commercial violent style and settled into the confines of gentle mysticism, Ren wondered why everyone sounded like NWA. Where were today's equivalents to "La-Di-Da-Di," "Eric B Is President" or *Criminal Minded?* he wondered. Today, everyone had a gimmick, drove low-riders in their videos, smoked weed, cavorted with naked women, bastardized the funk. "Even Tina Turner in her new shit. You seen it yet? And that's like—You know what I'm saying?!" He never dreamed that *Straight Outta Compton* would change hip-hop and American youth, and now that it did, he regretted it. To the point where, hearing people bump it in their rides, made him wince. *Straight Outta Compton* attracted the attention of the media: mainstream magazines attacked the group's "anti-police stance"; rap fanzines questioned their nihilistic agenda; the *Rolling Stones* and *Spins* considered them violent minstrels; the eggheads at the *Village Voice* deconstructed their music and searched for Oedipal subtexts, persecutory delusions and flawed logic.

After reviving every malignant stereotype about Blacks, Ren didn't understand why the media was hostile.

"The main thing was, New York had all'a the 'bomb' groups," he said apologetically. New York was the capital of the hip-hop world: KRS-One had the South Bronx; Public Enemy represented Long Island; Run-DMC promoted Hollis, Queens; Schoolly D covered Philadelphia; Ice-T tackled life in L.A.: "And all we was thinking, man—I ain't gonna lie, no matter what nobody in the group says—I think we all was thinking about making a name for Compton and L.A. That's why our first album, *Straight Outta Compton*, that's all you'll hear about."

Even though radio stations ignored the album and their first video got banned from MTV, the group toured. For once, here was a West Coast rap album that could hang with the sonic collages from East Coast groups Eric B and Rakim, BDP, Public Enemy, and Marley Marl: Instead of cheesy electropop, Dr. Dre was using the breakbeat albums we knew and loved, as well as state-of-the-art, Hank Shock-leesque arrangements. And their styles weren't so simple: this MC Ren kid, whoever he was, revealed a healthy KRS and Rakim influence, deviating from the group's caveman styles and dropping flows. Their breakbeats got them attention, their militancy got them into magazines, and their shows got them new fans. While on their first tour, they heard the album had sold 500,000 copies; soon after, the sales figure rose to 1,000,000. The video for "Express Yourself"—a positive song where Dre, before his pothead low-riding, proudly said he didn't smoke "weed or cess"—soon became an MTV favorite.

IV

"Well, why did you say this?" Ren remembers nasal-toned caucasian writers whining, viewing the group as a hip-hop Spinal Tap. They'd sit there staring, as writers asked, "What do you mean by this word?"

"And we used to be just saying any answer—bah bah bah bah— and acting stupid!"

While NWA—"a bunch of teenagers just tripping"—were trying to frighten white people, a white liberal audience soon adopted them as their latest Black group to support. Which is why *Spin*'s Mark Blackwell thought taking this poor Black group to the upscale Russian Tea Room and posing "tough questions" was such a great idea. In trying to show his readership that he could hang, Blackwell, however, soon found himself writing about how Ren threatened him with a beer bottle, an episode that made Blackwell's *Spin* feature more memorable.

But these were the NWA's glory days, similar to the Beatles' before they grew sideburns and John found Yoko; the group had their own sound and a loyal audience, multiplatinum sales and fat pockets. But then the drama. Things took a turn for the worse. Cube left the group and it hurt them, Ren admitted, but not enough to stop them from insulting him in interviews or on records. Shaking his head, Ren regretted telling Blackwell that Cube could suck his dick.

V

After Eazy contributed $2,500 to the Republican Party (a group diametrically opposed to NWA's politics) and attended a luncheon in Washington, D.C., for then President (and vitriolic racist) George

Bush, subsequent media reaction "got to his head," Ren continued.

By the time *Niggaz4Life* entered the pop charts at number two, then displaced Paula Abdul from the number one spot seven days later, "the world's most dangerous" (and successful) rap group was finished. NWA was a sinking ship, and Ren searched for a life preserver: the solo album he'd always wanted to record.

His label, Ruthless (owned by Eazy), felt an EP would be more appropriate, so Ren shrugged, penned a few lyrics and recorded them. Titled *Kiss My Black Azz*, the EP—which eventually sold a million copies within a year (a figure Cube reached overnight)—received lukewarm reviews.

Unhappy with his rushed work, Ren nonetheless toured to support it. He performed at the Apollo—where the audience thrilled to "Final Frontier" and, for a few days afterwards, took to wearing MC Ren T-shirts—and did a show or two in Hawaii. But that was it. Things slowed down and depression set in, the type that accompanies excessive drinking, weight gain and boredom, all of which plagued him at the time.

"I was just bored and it seemed like wasn't nothing in my life going right," he pensively nodded. This mental darkness resulted in "Same Old Shit," a song where a bored Ren chants, "Same ol' shit every day and every night / When it gets dark niggas get out of sight." He'd wake up, enter his Jeep, bump Marvin Gaye and "wish somebody would come out and have something to say" before DJ Train arrived bearing literature by Minister Louis Farrakhan and The Honorable Elijah Mohammed. The pivotal moment had arrived and with Islam, Ren reclaimed the spiritual center he lacked. Stripped by excessive drinking, guilt and feelings of worthlessness and inferiority, his self-confidence nevertheless returned.

Now he was positive, denounced the gangsta mentality and said things like, "See, a lot of fools think if you read, you're corny, but the more you read, the more you get in tune with yourself." A changed man, he would no longer rap about shooting niggas, fucking the police and slapping hoes. While he did have to put a bit of that on side one to make the album sell, he also slipped messages into songs like "Mayday on the Front Line" by couching them in familiar terms. "Uniting, putting guns together / To give white people stormy weather," was one ominous note. "Waiting for the day to get revenge on the days of the slave ships / we got the Bloods and the Crips," was another. The gangsta rapper abandoning his wool caps for an African crown was a stereotype, seen in *CB4* or the far superior *Fear of a Black Hat*—but Ren wasn't softening up. The violence was merely being directed at those who truly deserve it: "Oh my God, he's been shot in the chest / Yo, he's a redneck, huh / throw him with the rest / of the dead bodies we be burying / when two million niggas got guns and carry em."

VI

These days his troubled friendship with Eazy bothered him more than whether or not *Shock of the Hour* album would sell a zillion copies. During a recent visit to Audio Achievements, where E was completing his album, Ren found his friend surrounded by ass-kissing groupies, yes-men and, shadiest of all, aspiring artists. Eazy sat in the center, like an emperor and, visibly moved with jealous rage, studied every note on Dre's multiplatinum *The Chronic*. "Aw, it ain't all that," he yelled to his circus; "it ain't all that!" When Ren disagreed, the ass-kissers—many appearing on Eazy's recent work, *5150*—surrounded him.

"If you would've been there," Ren said, "you'd have seen everybody taking Eric's side."

Without Dre, Eazy failed to realize, NWA was over, Ren explained during heated arguments. Why promise *Rolling Stone* that NWA would have a new album by March, Ren asked. "How could you have NWA without Dre? How?!"

"We're gonna do it anyway! It's either . . . You gonna do it, be down or what?!"

"Man, I can't do no shit! It ain't gonna come out right—"

His friend's attitude towards Dre—the man most responsible for Eazy's success—appalled Ren. "A lot of people around him are probably saying, 'Fuck Dre,' and all this and that about me, but they weren't there in the beginning.

"The only relationship I have with Eazy," Ren disclosed, "is that I'm under contract to Ruthless Records. That's it. It ain't like we all 'homies' and shit because I just ain't got time. I don't want to get all deep into it because I'd rather, like, tell him the shit I got to say to his face."

For Eazy to attack Dre as a poseur, after sharing stages for years in NWA, was despicable—and hypocritical. "All people have to do is look at the stats," said Ren, knowing that any semblance of innocence on Eazy's part would be destroyed: "Look at Cube. He left. Dre left. And now look at how me and Eric's relationship is. Evidently something's wrong."

Chapter 9

Not Just a Jazz Thing

■

He was a happier person during the late 1980s. We met the night I drunkenly mounted the stage at Hotel Amazon, grabbed the mic and insulted all of the white girls in the audience. "You can all suck my dick," I yelled. "That's all you Devil bitches really want from niggas and spics!" Sometimes I think I must have been psychotic, using my dick to work my way into women's homes and finances. Mostly I tell myself I was just another teen wanting attention. Keith Elam, meanwhile, was an aspiring artist from Roxbury, Massachusetts, in the big city searching for a deal, and eager to make friends. "Your name's Ronin?" he asked.

We shook hands and became industry friends—greeting each other in clubs as if we'd been friends for a millenium. Outside of them, neither knew if the other had died. He returned people's calls back then, I remembered, wading through muddy snow and drinking a beer. The streets were dark and wet; the air was cold; it was a miserable night.

Three Gang Starr albums later, Keith was the center of attention in D&D Studios, where the interview was to be held and where there was an uproar. Keith was late and everyone was frantic. I caught a glimpse of him entering the studio like the hero in a John Woo film, as if he were moving in slow motion, wanting to avoid notice, needing a few minutes to regroup and prepare for this newest onslaught of attention. I raised my chin at this private person in greeting and in his response saw the final luminescence of youth on his face. "Sorry

I'm late," he said, his voice world-weary and cynical. He was drinking himself into true dissipation. Anyone could see this if they ran into him at the right club on a certain weekend. If he wasn't careful, the gleam would fade.

He disappeared around a corner, going further into D&D Studios. Voices rang through the air. The studio was as chaotic as a scene in a Robert Altman film; everyone had a job to do and most of the duties hinged on Keith's presence. Now that he was here, they pounced. The brown-bagged 40 in the folds of his black leather would have to wait. Although it was the eve of the release of *Hard to Earn,* the group's new album, his face looked like he just wanted to find a dark corner and drink his beer.

His DJ and producer Premier was in the studio working with Jeru Tha Damaja, and becoming difficult. A label publicist set upon Keith and pulled him to what he imagined was out of earshot. Keith had to speak with Premier, the publicist protested, calm him down and tell him to go along with the writers and photographers; this was important, the cover of *The Source* and now was not the time to pull this shit. The group needed this publicity, Keith was told, facing the ground, listening, occasionally nodding to show he understood: the *Source* cover would be great for album sales.

"I'll be right with you, Ronin," he sighed, trying his best to sound deferential, wondering if we were still cool or business associates.

Years ago, on boring hungover afternoons, we'd speak on the phone. During one call, he bragged about his new DJ, a kid from Texas. It was funny that I should be remembering this while waiting for him in a cramped lounge area. We'd drink at hip-hop clubs, get onstage, freestyle and try to pick up as many women as we could. My eyes scanned the KRS tags on the lounge's walls. After a night of drinking and rhyming, we'd ride the train in the early morning, discussing which girl we'd almost gotten to sleep with. It seemed like it happened a million years ago.

The studio outside was busy; arrangements were being made. After the interview, the group would accompany the *Source* photographer to the L train; they'd snap a few photos and choose the best for the cover. His buddies, a loud-talking bunch of hooligans who smoked weed, cursed and removed their shirts for amateur bodybuilding con-

Gangsta: Merchandising the Rhymes of Violence

tests ("Your arms ain't like mine! Look!"), began to filter into the room and take their seats.

■■

He sat there with a grim face, gripping the 40 tightly, and explained that his family were hardworking people, that his father broke the cycle of Elam men who held jobs in the construction industry. His father, he continued, didn't want to be a mechanic or a florist like his grandfather so he enrolled in law school.

In the background, Jeru Tha Damaja struggled with lyrics for "The Bitches." I peeked into the room and saw Premier hunched over a turntable, like a gargoyle over a precipice. He was scratching an NWA record, producing sounds that would make a listener imagine he was in a frenzy, but he had this stuff down to a science.

Sitting near me on a ratty couch, Keith drank from his beer and asked someone to shut the door; the noise was distracting and he might not want the label execs to see him drinking on the job.

"I have two uncles," he clarified. The first was a law student who worked to help pay his father's tuition. "And the other one: he works for the airlines," he said, a grin exploding onto his face.

"That's my uncle Charlie. He liked to drink Budweiser with the big fat stomach. Always pulling me real close so you could feel the stubble on his face and shit." He laughed; Charlie was an influence on him. His somnolent father wasn't as playful or understanding. "Charlie would be like [*gruffly*], 'Come here, come here, what are you doing?' "

The family, he firmly said, was tight-knit but competitive. His father was controlling, sensing that his son was going astray. He was constantly reminding him of the family's tradition of hard work. "Listen," Keith remembered him saying, "we worked hard to get where we got, and nobody could be in this household unless you responsible, which means, until you're old enough to start working, school is your job! You don't want to go to school? You ain't living here!"

His mother, a native of Trinidad, was the warmer parent, the more understanding one, the one with "feeling." While Mr. Elam attended law school, she worked as a librarian; when he graduated she returned to school for her master's degree. "They're both retired now but she lectures on Black children's literature. And"—he said proudly—"she was instrumental in getting all of the racist children's books taken off of the shelves in Boston."

During his teens as a high school student in Boston, he was exposed to bussing and race riots; the police beat him many times, he said. His parents were successful but refused to leave the old neighborhood. "See, they sent me to school in the suburbs and whatnot," he began, his voice still filled with resentment, "and every day, when I'd come back from school, kids around the way—" He stopped and turned to his homies, speaking to them as a coffeehouse poet would an intimate crowd: "You know how in East New York, Primo and them, their crib is like right across from Linden? And then it's private houses?" He faced me again, his eyes avoiding mine, somehow ashamed of revealing emotion; traces of hesitancy covered by self-confident words. "Every day I had to deal with kids who thought I had more than them. And they were trying to play me out. And I used to be mad at my pops for not putting me up on—like, talking me to about all that 'cause I had to learn that all on my own.

"First I was avoiding this kid," he said, adopting the down-home, simple approach authors like Claude Brown use in conveying childhoods in the inner city. "Then one day I had beef with Money. Next thing you know we were hanging, doing ill shit . . ." Keith had changed his view of the kid and made him a running partner. "Then I wasn't coming home from school and all that wild shit. And more and more it was mad rebelliousness.

"But now I understand my pops," he confessed; the generation gap slowly bridged. "It goes back to my grandfather. He was real quiet too, very serious, didn't talk to my pop that much." The grandfather, supposedly a somber fellow, should have gotten on well with Keith's father, as they were alike in temperament; but when the elder Elam wanted to speak, he approached Keith's rebellious uncle Charlie, the beer-drinking black sheep. "I guess their personalities were more alike and my father was more like the serious type."

It was ironic that Mr. Elam, who was studying to become a judge, had to fret over the company his son was keeping. Keith described him as a person who coldly held his emotions in check, who spoke out only to correct his wayward relatives and who couldn't stop him from associating with a teen named "Tee," a short budding pimp who called himself "Gang Star."

After borrowing his father's car, Keith would collect Tee and "go pick up his hoes and take 'em around," he explained. Behind the wheel, Keith learned the dynamics of street life. Young Tee would get out and approach women, asking for his money, and if they didn't have it, he'd commence to "sock 'em up." The women would be crying, appealing for mercy and Keith would sigh: It was none of his business; he was here with Tee, not to intervene. "It was a trip," he sighed, years later seeming to express no feeling.

Their escapades ended after one of their joyrides, when they tried unsuccessfully to rob a cab driver and Keith left the gun behind. Mr. Elam found it and his worst fears were confirmed. "My father used to always say things to me that I look back on as being good, but at the time used to make me mad. Like that expression, 'Nine broke niggas, you'll be the tenth one'? He used to be like, 'You and your friends, you're gonna grow up to be bums.' He didn't talk that much, but you knew when he was speaking, that he was upset for real.

"I did a lot of stuff to hurt him," he acknowledged. As his father predicted, many of his friends had fallen into drugs, graves or prison. "I had to leave them alone," Keith mourned. "I don't know what's up with them now but I hope they're all right," he said half convincingly. "That's not me: I smoke La, drink a couple of brews and that's it," he said, defending his honor.

■■■

After Boston was introduced to hip-hop—New Yorkers dropped tapes off with relatives—residents adopted cryptos like Ed O.G. and RSO and created a local music scene. Keith started to rhyme, and with his friend Big Shug performed at parties. He met the Harvard "Herbs" who would create *The Source* at WHRB parties.

Freestyling, battling and human beat-boxing were in vogue and Keith—ignoring the family tradition—immersed himself into the culture. This was the life of the street, not the mind, he thought, until a Run-DMC lyric provided absolution.

" 'After twelfth grade I went straight to college,' " Keith recited, accentuating words exactly as DMC had done on "Sucker MCs."

"That shit influenced me. That line right there 'cause my peeps wanted me to go to college and all that but I wanted to MC. Once I heard that, I was like, 'Damn, he did both.' That's my shit."

After stealing his friend Tracy's nickname—"Add another r and that'll be some fat shit," he remembered thinking, nodding conspiratorially—an early lineup was assembled: his friend Shug, a kid named Damo-D-Ski and a DJ named 1-2–B-Down, who could afford equipment and allowed them to practice at his home.

Other MCs visited; battles were held, rivalries developed and songs were written. But Keith made one of his quick decisions and felt that leaving Boston, going solo, would be the only way to succeed. His music would "only go so far" if he stayed; he'd be a "local yokel."

"I never wanted to be just a diamond in the neighborhood," he said coldly, ambition raging in his heart. "That wasn't enough."

It was 1982, the day after Christmas, and he told himself, "I'm out.

"I'm gonna do this thing," he thought, packing his bags and preparing for the big move to New York, where he would struggle for four years—the length of a presidential term—before getting a deal.

As Keith spoke, Shug nodded. He was one of the friends in Boston who had fulfilled Mr. Elam's prophecy. "You and your friends, you're gonna grow up to be bums," Mr. Elam had said. Shug had indeed been arrested and sentenced to time in the Charles Street prison and at Walpole State.

Upon his release two years ago, a very different Keith than the one he left behind put Shug in the "Take It Personal" video. Keith was also helping him start a career of his own, and making him part of something called the Gang Starr Foundation. "That's my crew," Keith slurred, the alcohol and weed beginning to take hold. "I met Melachi when he was twelve; he's seventeen now. I been building with him. He's like a philosopher, a scholar; we had a lot in common, passing concepts back and forth.

"Dap is like the brother I never had. We used to go everywhere together. When you saw me, you saw him. Jerue is a person I build with. The Foundation are guys that I freestyle with all the time." Many of his friends, I noticed, were affiliated with the Lo-Lifes, a Brooklyn gang who literally robbed the shirt off of someone's back if it were Ralph Lauren, particularly Polo.

He didn't discuss his college years: he chose to skillfully downplay them in front of his friends. Nothing was more damaging to a hip-hop career then being seen as an intelligent artist. "Intelligent artists" were labeled "alternative" and maligned as bourgeois dilettantes. But the fact remained that he had graduated from college and had been able to hold a position as a social worker during the early eighties.

He lived in a number of New York areas — East New York, Bedford-Stuyvesant (on "Malcolm X and Quincy"), Harlem, Queens and the Bronx — before quietly deciding that Brooklyn was right for him. Founded in 1646 as the small Dutch village of Breukelen, he felt at home in the second-largest and most-populated New York borough. In the early lonely days, before he fell in with his current crowd, he'd see Biz Markie shopping at Albee Square Mall, or Big Daddy Kane "when he used to live on Lewis." If they could make it, so could he.

"But I was never like a lot of kids now who just want to hang around and stuff and keep telling you 'I got this demo' or 'Listen to my freestyle,' " he angrily pointed out. "They don't understand!" he yelled. "This is some shit! It takes hard work and dues and a method!"

He'd never forget the early days in stores like Downstairs Records, Rock & Soul, and Music Factory. He wouldn't buy anything; he simply wanted to be near the music; he wanted to see the artists who occasionally dropped in. He drew inspiration from seeing them browse through the racks.

In Downstairs Records, they hung out in the rear of the store, where Nick, the owner, had a turntable set up. It was there for customers interested in hearing what they were buying, but most times was used by kids with spare time who wanted to hear breakbeats for free. The knowledgeable staff — most of them aspiring producers themselves — could be seen hunting for drum breaks and bass lines when the store was empty. When it was full, they debated the state of modern hip-hop with regulars like Hank Shocklee, Biz Markie or Marley Marl, who, in addition to their opinions, were also often the recipients of their newest musical discoveries. Public Enemy once considered recording a song called "Language of the Enemy" to one of the beats Ill Will discovered. It was said that he was partly responsible for most of hip-hop's biggest hits.

Aspiring artists like Keith, hungry for deals and willing to work for them, would stand by the record racks, pulling out pens and copying label information from album covers. They'd have the address and phone number for a favorite label, and would either call or drop their demo off in person. Today, getting a deal had become too easy. One person said a good word and you were in; smoke a few bones with an exec and you were in; hang around and kiss someone's ass and you were in. Get a deal, bite someone's style and watch the label buy praise with full-page advertisements. And you were in.

Nobody handed Keith his deal, he wanted readers to know. I listened intently as he described the jobs he took after arriving to the city. After a stint in construction like the other Elams before his father and uncle entered law school, Keith applied for a mailroom position. "With a college degree working in a mailroom," he grievously reflected. "That's wack!!! But I had to do that." His only salvation was his Walkman, constantly rewinding Queen Latifah's first single "Wrath of My Madness," and having faith that moving to New York was not the mistake everyone said it was.

Before his deal, he performed at clubs like Hotel Amazon, Payday, Milky Way, Fever, Devil's Nest, Zodiac, Rooftop, Union Square and Latin Quarter, back when going to a hip-hop club meant dancing, meeting girls, making friends and discussing new music. There were fights — some clubs were worse than others — but not as many as today. Hip-hop fans weren't suckers back then; you'd rarely see ten people jumping someone. Girls were girls and men were men; people drank, danced, smiled and hit dark corners to freestyle against other MCs. Keith arrived in New York during the era of the truly noteworthy hip-hop song. Public Enemy shocked the planet with *Nation of Millions*, Stetsasonic were in the midst of a string of hits ("Go Stetsa," "Sally"), Ultramagnetic dropped "Ego Trippin,'" the Audio Two had "Top Billin,'" and Superlover Cee and Casanova Rud crowded dance floors with "Do the James" and "Supercasanova."

You'd see groups make unscheduled appearances in tiny clubs, like when Ultra challenged then-new De La Soul to a battle at Hotel Amazon, and De La mysteriously disappeared after performing "Plug Tuning." Or Hank Shocklee holding a glass of ice water, standing on the edge of the dance floor, coldly eyeing the crowd, determining which songs kept people moving. He'd mentally deconstruct a popular favorite to its basic elements; then he'd inject those elements into another Public Enemy hit. These were the good days, hip-hop's Golden Age when everything clicked and the music brought people together. Not like today's bullshit, which relies on fabricated nihilism and misanthropy.

Wild Pitch Records was a small, newly formed mom-and-pop operation run by Stu Fine, when Keith, after a four-year struggle, signed with them. With DJ Mark the 45 King, he flirted with nationalism on four songs ("Gusto," "Knowledge," "Moving On," and "Bust a Move"). He was proud to be intelligent back then: he was optimistic, young and eager; his music was built on breakbeats but fortified by Mark's keen jazz sense.

"[We used] jazz horns and [cut] them up 'cause everybody was on the James Brown samples," Keith said. However experimental the four songs were, they sadly failed to find more than a local audience.

Keith spent afternoons at the label's offices, perusing incoming demos and suggesting that Stu Fine sign artists like Lord Finesse and the Inner Circle Posse. "When I heard Premier's demo, it was so fat because the guy"—he never mentioned Stu by name—"told me he was doing it on a four-track." When he was offered a position as an in-house producer, Inner Circle member Premier—aka Christopher Martin—instead expressed interest in meeting Keith.

A correspondence began and Keith began receiving tapes from Premier in his mail. This was when Keith called and happily told me about Premier. Premier had recently graduated from Prairie View University, just outside of Houston, and would soon be returning to the city. He didn't want to live with his father in East New York ("and he can explain that to you when you talk to him"), so he moved into Keith's apartment in the Fordham section of the Bronx. It was four A.M. when he pulled up in "an old blue truck with the fat system that Premier put together" and began unloading crates of records. The crates dominated much of the one-room studio apartment, leaving space only for a futon mattress, and made it so cramped that when one had a girl coming over, they'd tell the other, "Yo, man, here's five dollars! Go get a chicken sandwich or something. . . ."

The background music—Jeru's track—abruptly ended, announcing that Premier had completed the session. The air was thick with tension when he entered, sat down across from Keith, reclined and ignited a thick blunt. His eyes were hard and his face was sceptical.

Keith was explaining how, for their first album, the aptly titled *No More Mr. Nice Guy*, they were under a tight deadline. They had to have an album written and recorded in two and a half weeks. His feelings about it were mixed, he admitted: Part of him saw it as a demo— "an introduction 'cause it was just the beginning and stuff hadn't really evolved"—and part felt that "classic songs came out of that album that weren't marketed the greatest."

Keith made another abrupt change and left Wild Pitch for larger label Chrysalis, an EMI subsidiary with stronger promotion power. Their career began to take off—their second album, *Step Into the Arena*, was a more focused work—but a nasty rumor began to circulate in the industry. They had visited their label's offices, to settle a business deal, with a handgun. When I inquired about this, Keith eyed me coldly and said, "We won't talk about that." He was a stranger now.

"It's dead," Premier grimly added.

"But did this happen?" I probed.

"I'll say this," he demanded. "Everything's cool, we're still there and all is well."

▎◀eith sat there listening to Premier explain why the press had labeled Gang Starr "jazz rappers"; he stared at the carpet in front of his feet. The room filled with blue smoke. We covered all of the basics in a hip-hop interview—tour experiences, their future, feelings on the new album, their jazz rap image—then Keith said, "I think that some of the media—not all of it—and Hollywood, fucked the rap game up by putting different labels on the music: like jazz rap, gangsta rap and political rap. There's really no such thing as all of that. It's either real, authentic, fat beats, skills . . ."

This led into an animated discussion of noteworthy hip-hop: Jeru Tha Damaja's "Come Clean" was a favorite. Another was Nasty Nas,

Gangsta: Merchandising the Rhymes of Violence

the young Queens protégé whose intricate lyrics evoked Rakim in his prime. "To me, he sounds like nobody else," said Premier, producer of two Nas tracks. "He got his own little pimp style. There's mad examples."

Premier's voice would be deemed overconfident, arrogant even, by a casual listener, but, after paying dues, it was of natural consequence that he would sound like this. Once a marginal figure, his sound had become one of hip-hop's best. Outside production work had elevated him onto the A-list; artists willing to pay top dollar for a track sought him out; critics hailed his achievements. After years of cutting people off, for the sake of his success, Keith found himself in a position where he might be the one dismissed, and awareness of his situation showed on his face.

Between Gang Starr albums, Keith had released *Jazzmatazz*, a jazz-rap fusion with live musicians, and in addition to low sales, it received lukewarm reviews. Premier meanwhile had teamed with Branford Marsalis for the critically acclaimed Buckshot Le Fonque album. Both had been outside jazz projects but Premier's had outdone Keith's.

Keith had produced for Neneh Cherry and Salt-N-Pepa, but Premier had produced for heavyweights KRS-One, Nice & Smooth, Heavy D, Jeru, and Nas. Keith would start a production company while Premier would begin work on a remix for Sinead O'Connor, then work on tracks for the Lady Rage.

As Premier spoke, I felt sad for Keith, eclipsed by the temperamental man who now held the cards. The tables had turned; Keith was now on the receiving end.

"You got to stay focused on what people like, what you like and then you got to compare and be able to hang in that same area as all of those other records," said Premier of his formula for successful production. "But"—he stressed—"you don't have to sound like those records."

"Like Wu-Tang," said Keith from the sidelines. "That don't sound like nobody."

"But that shit is dope," the DJ corrected. "Same with Black Moon."

"Same with Snoop . . ."

"Yeah, his shit's for real," he told Keith in a fatherly tone. "I don't want my record to sound like that, but his records are dope. That's their style. They know what they're doing. We know what we're doing."

After a pause, he added M.O.P. to the list. " 'How About Some Hardcore' is one of the dopest records out now."

"Wu-Tang album," a neglected Keith restated.

"The style of production," Premier continued, silent all these years and now in a position to speak. "They got all different styles. You know when each MC is on. Some people say Method Man sound like Busta [Rhymes, Leaders of the New School], but they different. There's a lot of people with scruffy voices."

"It made me feel good to see Rakim and them come back like that," Keith agreed. "We used to see them around the way all the time," he said, reminding Premier that they were a team.

"I like Ice Cube's album too," the DJ continued.

"That shit is fat," said Keith, still trying to keep up. "I like 'They Won't Call Me a Nigga When I Get to Heaven.' That reminds me of KRS-One. 'Higher Level.' That shit he's kicking."

How about the Lench Mob's first album, I asked, smoking a cigarette and wanting to hear from both.

"That was dope," yelled Premier, making Keith sulk and direct his attention to his bottle.

We walked into the studio next door, and Premier turned a few knobs on the mixing board. Gang Starr's entourage crowded in. A gentle bass groove washed over us and Keith's voice told aspiring MCs, "This shit ain't easy. If you ain't got it you ain't got it." It was an acrid statement to make, somewhat cruel, but Keith had become a different person when success arrived. He had distanced himself from whoever stood in his way, and achieved the success he used to dream of; and now that he was here, surrounded by the ass kissers, and paid from his record deal, fuck anyone that wasn't down with him.

After "Alongwaytogo" a noise track that suggested a funkier Onyx, Premier, doing all of the talking now, introduced "Code of the Streets," a song Keith produced. "We did this for *Poetic Justice* but they didn't accept it," he shrugged; I sensed tension in the group. Before Premier joined the group, DJ the 45 King would tell Keith, "You don't need me to do your beats, you can do 'em yourself." Premier

Gangsta: Merchandising the Rhymes of Violence

was outshining Keith, gaining a name for himself, and he didn't seem to take Keith's production seriously. I heard many songs that evening but these—including Keith's "Code of the Streets"—were the ones that stood out in my mind, these and "Speak Ya Clout," which again teamed the group with Jeru and Lil' Dap.

After Jeru's verse, Dap rhymed over a dark bass line. As he spoke, I could picture the Brooklyn neighborhoods he described—bustling crowds, cops on corners, and confrontations. When the last song ended, Keith shut the tape machine off. Premier had already left by then, he had to move his parked car or get a ticket. Keith seemed saddened by his departure; he couldn't wait until the interview was over.

We walked into another room, away from the crowd, and I asked how he was doing, my voice implying I was asking how he was really doing and not for the showbiz answer. His demeanor changed; he let his guard down, sat on a chair and said, "Alright." The bravado and coldness left: We were two old friends seeing each other for the first time in years; the first time our paths ever crossed on a professional level, with me "Ronin Ro of *The Source*," and him "Guru from Gang Starr." I was happy for his success, he deserved it; wished him well with the album, told him I liked it and would support it in print. He thanked me and said, "Premier came up with the album title *Hard to Earn,* meaning that true respect and longevity is hard to earn."

His face looked heavy, tired and a little blue. It had been a busy day—editing a video and coordinating a *Source* cover shoot, drinking Budweiser as his uncle Charlie once did—and it was late. He had to finish the interview and pack up—there was still the trip home, and tomorrow would be another day filled with questions, photos, the entourage, getting high, label employees, phone calls. "Anything that you want is hard to earn," my old friend said, sounding none too happy.

Chapter 10

Falling Off

It was a bleak snowy night in New York, and the wind, howling through empty streets, seemed to be cursing. Members of the group Whodini were seated at a thick wooden table in Hoolihan's, an over-lit pub in the Empire State Building that catered mostly to yuppies, tourists and budget-minded couples and adulterers. "Everything's still in effect," said Ecstasy, older now, and not wearing his black sombrero—the group's trademark when white people loved them. He was discussing his group's low-key comeback attempt through an appearance on Terminator X's radio-friendly "It All Comes Down to the Money," they had sparked renewed interest in them. But they were reentering a hip-hop dominated by G-funk gangsta rap and a vast East Coast underground that included the Wu-Tang Clan, Gang Starr and Nas.

So being on the comeback trail meant staying humble. They had to conduct themselves like presidential candidates: no hand was too clammy to shake, no question too pointless to answer, no promise too ambitious to make, no infant too ugly to kiss. Their trendy hip-hop outfits did nothing to lighten their obvious solemnity. Their weathered faces genealogically confirmed their status as a branch of the Old School.

The hip-hop world had changed—snappy responses that once charmed white interviewers during the 1980s no longer achieved the desired effect—so they altered their responses to try to conform to the strange new world. Studying the industry from the periphery had provided a basic understanding of what was expected of hip-hop stars today.

The veterans had ended their photo shoot for *Rap Pages* and silently paced on the wooden floor of the loft. Their publicist—a young white girl in faded jeans and black boots—schmoozed with the mulatto lensmen. There was new business to attend to and Whodini knew their place: they were old-timers who took the backseat to newer acts in her caseload.

A merciless snowstorm had rendered the studio almost unreachable. Arriving, I was greeted by the sight of the publicist marching around, barking orders as vehemently as Sawako had in Tokyo. With drooping, spiritless eyes, Whodini observed her. Morale was low. Depression settled over them. Down on their luck, they were in no position—for the time being at least—to do anything but yield to her wishes. If she wanted to speak with these photographers and make Whodini wait, they simply had to accommodate her. Their former publicists would never have treated them so rudely, but their former publicists, they remembered, were no longer in business. This brash new firm—run by the assistants and interns of their former representers—was the only legitimate company that would deal with them. Whodini would do anything as long as the firm—and this dopey, young white girl—accomplished something.

In an empty corner, I guzzled my 40 and hoped it would fend off the cold. Chuckling, with a chill still bouncing around in my bones, I stared at the people in the studio. The photographers stood listening to the white girl, posing as self-consciously as the models they worked with. Their flunkies stirred a pot of chicken boiling over on the stove and changed tapes in the portable radio.

As the lensmen attacked their stew, the group's eyes began to water. No one asked if they were hungry; it was as if they were orphans watching nobles at the dinner table. I almost expected them to cup their palms and beg, "More, please, sir," as Oliver Twist had done in the Dickens classic. Resisting temptation, they maintained their dignity; they stuck close to each other as if they were the only friends they had in the world, as realization crept in. During the photo shoot, the photographers had spoken of how they were big fans and wished them

Gangsta: Merchandising the Rhymes of Violence

well; but the group came to accept that, to the photographers and all in attendance, they were simply the six-o'clock photo shoot.

An assistant stopped the music; with a tap of a finger, Whodini's hopeful new single had been replaced with Kenny G's insipid "jazz."

■■

With each passing second, I began to hate this publicist more and more. Something about her brought out the worst in a man. I'd met her type so many times in this industry. White kids who attended downtown clubs and surrounded themselves with dark Black faces: citing the "many advances" made by the civil rights movement and name-dropping "Martin" and "Malcolm" as if they were close personal friends of the family. Conversation tended to veer towards modern politics, even if they had to steer it there, so that these white devils could offer their obligatory joke about Al Sharpton's hairstyle. Why did hip-hop groups always discuss race? these crackers would ask, with as much sincerity as they could bolster. Couldn't these Blacks see that it just made matters worse?

They'd stand near you in faded blue jeans, Pumas and Kangols, discussing the Old School as if they'd invented it. When they arrived at the velvet ropes outside of what purported to be a hip-hop club, they waved blond dreadlocks at the discriminating doorman and were immediately admitted. It was rare when they'd glance at their Black and Latino friends on line and say, "I'll see you inside, alright?" For them Black people were like children. They were so warm and friendly, they felt. They were so oppressed and so musical.

That ass-kissing Blacks liked to be around them was irrefutable proof, however, that these hip-hop whiteys were *different* from their suburban racist relatives, former neighbors or schoolmates. Acceptance from Uncle Tom Blacks confirmed these whiteys' inherent sense of *soul*. They knew every prevailing dance (the "kid *n* play") or slang term ("Hey, chill out!"), and could tell you more than you ever wanted to know about Richard Wright, James Baldwin or any other Black writer whose book was displayed in the African bookstore. And if you mentioned James Brown? Shit. They'd chew your ear off, regaling you for hours with knowledge gleamed from tomes, biographies, liner notes or *Vibe* magazine. They'd infer, in their most reverential tone, that being white and well-studied meant they could more fully appreciate a Black artist. Black audiences, they believed, did not know where their race's true genius lie.

"Kris Kross's new album's fat as hell," they'd intone, before standing silent, sipping their beer and eyeing any passing Black girl, waiting for us to shuck, jive and say, "Well, tha's mighty good, white boy!" And this young, white college grad who had somehow become Whodini's publicist was no different. But people like her were, sadly, always awarded with the most vital positions in this industry.

"Fuck that ho," I yelled, lighting a Newport, ready at that moment to storm off and make her look like the horse's ass to her Black employers. By her cold stare, I felt that she viewed us as subhuman scum, unworthy of being in the same loft. To her, my homie Dig Doug and I were uncouth, a bit too cavalier in hooded sweats and jeans, gulping from bottles, the dregs of society unfit for polite company.

"But we're here to see Whodini," I reassured Dig, as my finger swept across the room like a rifle. "And all these Tom motherfuckers can eat a dick! They have nothing to do with hip-hop! If it weren't for the artists, they wouldn't have jobs! These are the motherfuckers who pimp the music!"

Overhearing me, she grew visibly upset. "We're going to Hoolihan's," she scowled. "You can come if you want," she said, her tone implying she wished I'd burn in hell.

After standing near our table, awaiting an order, the waiter scurried off with his pad. Frozen by that blizzard outside, I sipped from a bottle of beer and regarded my hands. Stiff as wood—red and throbbing—they were solid enough to crash through a table. The wind outside had made my dry face feel as if a juvenile had carved it with a boxcutter.

Former "sex symbol" Ecstasy was explaining that his childhood had been normal. "Fine, childish, athletic, adolescent . . . just a normal childhood that you would have in Brooklyn. No different than anybody else."

"We came up like people in the projects come up," the former project resident continued. "The best way you can." Instead of milking his upbringing for ghetto credibility, Ecstasy's bonhomie evoked

Gangsta: Merchandising the Rhymes of Violence

memories of the good-hearted characters in *Good Times*. Unlike Run-DMC—who enlisted Pete Rock for a comeback and adopted a contemporary urban "attitude"—Ecstasy aspired to again be the calm voice in the maelstrom. "You have a mom, a pop, brothers and sisters, and go through normal family behavior," he said sarcastically, his eternal patience—necessary for a successful comeback—wearing as thin as the heels on his shoes.

After ordering dinner—one platter of appetizers—the group's DJ, Grandmaster Dee, mentioned that he had been athletic. During his school years, he played tag, baseball and basketball, back when the streets were safe. "They had Boys' Clubs," he said wistfully, "and they had unity back then. Everybody stuck together."

Everybody but the Tomahawks, Hellcats, Jolly Stompers, Brooklyn Bachelors, Black Spades and the many other gangs that comprised the 315 infiltrating New York City during that era. "That was when New York was going through their period," Ecstasy restated, dismissing the topic and the past with an urgent wave of his palm, the topic of gangs in the early seventies far more intriguing, and sure to outshadow their comeback story.

"Back in them days, you played baseball, basketball or you played football, man!" Ecstasy lamented. "I don't see kids out here trying to play that much anymore. . . . Not in the projects, anyway." Today's kids had no social programs or afterschool activities so the hierarchy of the streets was warping their values.

Grandmaster Dee, once a member of Brooklyn's Jolly Stompers, said it wasn't until the recently departed Master Don introduced him to hip-hop that he felt alive. "May he rest in peace," he said of his former schoolmate, detailing how, in 1976, he attended jeans with Don that were held by the Disco Twins in Queensbridge Park.

Ecstasy's inspiration came from baritoned pioneers Grandmaster Flowers, the Disco Enforcers, and Frankie Dee; and from the countless number of lesser-known headliners at local jams. "I heard somebody back in the days—when I was young—do a little nursery rhyme and I said, 'Damn,' " he confessed. "I just thought that shit was so incredible." He personalized the nursery rhymes and hoped to become as famous as Grandmaster Flash and the Furious Five or the Funky Four + One More, the legends that his group later outsold.

Sipping from a clear glass of water, Jalil ignored the soft Muzak

Falling Off

piped into the dining area and said that he also attended outdoor fetes in Brooklyn. "But my major influence was DJ Hollywood, a Queens-Uptown rapper that was down with Eddie Cheba and DJ June Bug." Hollywood, a loud, jaw-flapping crowd-pleaser, was credited with adding the term *hip-hop* to the music's argot, during the days when he yelled at crowds between acts at the Apollo.

Before there was a group, there was Jalil, he wanted me to know. He was an aspiring rapper who forced himself to stay awake so that he could hear the *Mr. Magic Rap Attack* radio show on WHBI. Magic rented time from the station and sold commercials to pay for it, and his show—broadcast from one to five A.M. every Thursday morning—invented rap radio as we know it. Decades before Polly-O String Cheese or Sprite asked Daddy-O or A Tribe Called Quest to promote their products, Magic's commercials featured popular breakbeats of the day.

One night, Jalil phoned Magic, told him about his group. Magic expressed interest in hearing a radio promo from them. Set to the "Theme from S.W.A.T.," Whodini's first demo was aired three times a night; their first demo cemented Jalil and Magic's friendship.

When Magic was hired by larger station WBLS-FM, Jalil tagged along. "Then a company from Europe contacted him and wanted to make a record about him because they knew he was the premier DJ to play rap on the radio," Jalil recalled. The company was Jive ("a little company out of London, England," they said, resentful at the label they'd helped to build) and the song was "Magic's Wand."

Jalil was contracted to do the record. But it was a testament to his kindness that, on the morning of the recording session, he traveled to Ecstasy's neighborhood and told his old friend to accompany him. Astonished that Jalil was making a record, Ecstasy assisted with the crowd replies in the background. He felt a little jealous until Jalil asked, "Yo, man, you wanna rhyme?" He definitely wanted to, but answered, "Yo, they ain't gonna let me!" Jalil responded, "Watch," and coached him on how to recite certain vocals.

"They picked it up, his voice was on there, it's in the house, it's going out," he rushed. "Boom! We splitting the points, we down, Whodini's in focus now."

"So we did that track and they shipped it to New York and it was only a single deal at that time," Ecstasy continued for him, somewhat

Gangsta: Merchandising the Rhymes of Violence

embarrassed, "and then they was like, 'It took off good.' "

Whodini were offered an album deal, and recorded "The Haunted House of Rock," a commercialized knockoff of Kurtis Blow's "Christmas Rappin'." They hoped that their own holiday theme would equal Blow's success and make it one of those songs radio loved to play when the holiday season advanced.

They were Magic protégés then, outsiders with lackluster hip-hop tracks and limited connections until Magic introduced Jalil to Russell Simmons and Russell introduced the group to Larry Smith, the producer working wonders with Run-DMC. The smooth, sophisticated Whodini image was sculpted—cowboy hats and blazers would provide a necessary contrast—and the R&B sound was crafted. Described by David Top as "an R&B man," producer Smith—the man most responsible for their creative breakthrough, *Escape*—captured Whodini's many strengths. The album yielded the classic hits "Friends," "Big Mouth," and "The Freaks Come Out at Night," defining hip-hop's middle, commercial age and inspiring many imitators. Theirs was the sound of the early 1980s, when MCs selected specific targets—liars, loudmouths, greedy friends, perverts—and humorously attacked them. Verses were short and ended with memorable hooks. Instead of DJs cutting up breakbeats, session players provided glossy music, which attracted white ears and wallets.

Never as "hard" as Run-DMC or LL Cool J, Whodini's trilogy nonetheless managed to earn them a permanent position in hip-hop history. They traveled the world with the Fresh Fest Tour; huge audiences sang their every word; their videos were regularly aired on every important music program; they appeared on a multitude of magazine covers; critics everywhere sang their praises—even KRS-One admitted asking himself, "When will I be large like Whodini?"

Then more and more new groups began to release product and Whodini's disappearance didn't matter. Like the Fat Boys, they lacked the necessary edge to compete with younger MCs like Big Daddy Kane and Biz Markie. Public tastes were shifting towards more street-oriented music but Whodini were trapped in a time warp. Hip-hop was too progressive, they failed to see. The sound they had just perfected had already become outdated.

They sat at the table and smiled warmly, content with the memories of the good times and of their contributions. It would have been unfair to bring up the part they played in introducing the "ballad rap." After Whodini released "One Love," a slow-paced love rap promising wine, candlelight and flowers to a loved one, MC Shan released the dewy-eyed "Left Me Lonely." Soon after, LL wrote "I Need Love," sold millions, and solidified the ballad rap's position as an obligatory annoyance on most hip-hop albums released during that more innocent era.

■■■

"It all comes down to the money / whether its rainy or snowy or sunny / Funny but it all comes down to the money / admit it, I'm in it for the cash, I'm in it for the cash . . ."
—Whodini, "It All Comes Down to Money"

Only when Old School nostalgia became the trend did anyone consider Whodini's fate. Speculation attributed their absence to drug use or flawed material. Jalil shook his head, looked wounded and angry then sighed. "It's a long story, it's a real long story," he wearily began. "It's more than one element."

They left Jive records when the label refused to "double up" their points during a contract negotiation. "We felt that it was time to stop bullshitting." At MCA, they encountered deeper troubles. "We had a good situation that turned bad and we walked right into a bad situation." They were viewed as "tax write-offs," Jalil claimed; he described an ongoing feud between MCA's pop and R&B departments. When Whodini signed, both sides wanted to be solely responsible for promoting their *Bag of Tricks* album. He made them sound like the two women who once brought a baby to wise King Solomon. Both women wanted the baby. Solomon suggested they cut it in half.

There was no King Solomon at MCA Records so *Bag of Tricks* became the sole casualty of the bickering. The pop department felt they had a crossover album; R&B promotion felt slighted. The pop department should stick to New Edition; the R&B department wouldn't hit Top 40. It was interesting, I thought, that no one considered *Bag of Tricks* a rap album.

"Whoever's saying that [about drug use] doesn't know what I just kicked to you about the business side," Jalil said more intensely.

Gangsta: Merchandising the Rhymes of Violence

It was common industry belief that they'd fallen off due to inflated egos, crossover material, and drug use, and still he denied it. No, Jalil protested. Whoever spread that objectionable rumor did not understand. Machiavellian plots had been hatched against them by promotion people at MCA Records. In fact, it was larger than that, he explained with wide and glassy eyes. The Japanese may have been involved! The interlopers had invented the CD player as a means of dominating the worldwide electronics field, he insisted. These tawny fiends made it impossible for anyone to hear music on anything but this more expensive device. Whodini's music should have been released on the more affordable vinyl or cassette format, he stated, but the Japanese bosses put it out on CD.

And if it wasn't this, well, then, it must have been secret high-level corporate espionage! Perhaps these faceless Japanese bosses needed their newest purchase, MCA, to show a profit loss. By doing this, they would actually make money, he explained.

He had lost me.

And one of the ways this profit was earned? he continued. By underpromoting albums by Whodini, Ralph Tresvant, and Eric B and Rakim—all Black musicians, mind you. But no, he concluded with a straight face: it was absolutely untrue that drug use was a factor in Whodini's Olympian fall from grace.

Days later, *The Source's* Robert Marriott quoted the group discussing their drug use. ("We weren't angels," Ecstasy told him then. "We were young and wild.")

Now this is what I mean. The group was past their prime in 1994, hip-hop's year of the Gat, grimy style, Death Row Records and Wu-Tang Clan, and they were mouthing off about which groups were wack and which had no right to exist. They ignored the fact that, although they were back in the limelight with "It All Comes Down to the Money," and their video was aired on The Box, the song was on Terminator X's album. They didn't even have a record deal!

A bunch of sad-faced clowns, they trooped through a blizzard on the prostitute-ridden West Side. The walk was as solemn as a death march. We reached Thirty-fourth and had to trudge six or seven additional blocks across town to reach an economically priced meat-and-potatoes pub in the Empire State Building. Their publicist hadn't even offered to call them a cab.

I nursed a warm can of Bud and trailed behind. Jesus, it was cold. Snow slapped my cheeks; slush dirtied my sneakers. Tree branches were shaking in the howling wind. This was pretty down-and-out, having to stumble through sub-zero cold during one of the city's most frenzied snowstorms. Whatever happened to the limos?

We'd have to walk faster or the interview would be cut short. Jalil, I believe, had to be at work tomorrow, fresh and well-rested. The entourage didn't want to wait for their subway all night. Things were bad for them. In a day or two, they'd interrupt their "new beginning" and board a bus in front of the Apollo. With Melle Mel, the Treacherous Three and other old-timers, Whodini were part of a package tour heading for Jersey and Philadelphia.

IV

So now they sat in the warm pub waiting for another plate of appetizers, drinking water when they may have wanted soda, and waiters had begun to turn off the lights, their roundabout signal that everyone should now go home. Their publicist was a bit of a Scrooge, calculating who ordered what, so I neglected to pay for my beers.

After leaving MCA—Jalil continued in a dreamy tone, the kind you hear in old films before the picture loses focus and they head into a flashback—they landed at Arista. They should have known that this was Whitney Houston's label, and that Arista would never release threatening street music. For some reason, despite overwhelming evidence that hip-hop was heading in a harder direction, they recorded the gentle *Open Sesame*. When they discovered that hip-hop fans now wanted to dance to faster beats, they threw in the towel. They had been in London again, where they recorded all of their albums, and failed to keep up with current trends. "Kane had dropped 'I Get Raw' and P.E. was like 'Bring the Noise,' " Jalil shrugged, the pain burning like fire in his pupils. "We were burned down by then."

The business disputes, and negative reviews—not to mention yellow espionage—took their toll. Whodini couldn't accept that they had brought about their own downfall; that their music had strayed too far from the streets; that their commercial sense alienated hardcore fans; that their lyrics had grown too lustrous; that cocaine had induced dissipation.

Gangsta: Merchandising the Rhymes of Violence

The compounding problems caused tension and group members were soon at each other's throats. Only time apart would help mend the wounds, I was told. "You always hurt the one you love, and that's what happened," he said regretfully, sounding as he did on one of his love ballads. "That's what caused a minor separation amongst us, but love overrules all," he continued in the same vein. "We'd see each other. We shared too much together. We refused to let it go out like that. We owed ourselves more than that." He made it sound like a foreign film's doomed romance.

"We owe the Creator more than that," he said, as if only God could bring them together, when it was actually Terminator X, whose invitation to appear on a song miraculously caused the hungry trio to bury the hatchet. They were eternally grateful that Terminator, who had been "wet behind the ears" when the famous Whodini taught him how to tour, would remember his old pals.

They were "nervous at first," and worried about reuniting with "wild" Larry Smith but eventually penned lyrics for Terminator's topic and saw "It All Comes Down to the Money" resurrect their dead career. But they didn't want to be called "legends." The adjective implied that one's best work was behind him.

In 1994, Old School artists were returning in droves, nostalgia was in full swing and the equivalent of a Vegas circuit was developing. Newer MCs saying "yes yes y'all," "you don't stop," and many other clichés convinced the old-timers that now would be a perfect time for a mass comeback. The Treacherous Three regrouped for an album, and the Fearless Four were preparing their own, but the Old Schoolers were overestimating the depth of the youth's pool of nostalgia. They wanted the clichés, but without the posturing, bitterness or shitty attitudes displayed by many Old Schoolers. Too many old-timers would say, "We started this music!"

There was nothing else to discuss. It was late; there was work to be done in the morning. They had to rehearse the old moves and memorize the old lyrics for their upcoming show. It was sad but inevitable that certain groups, to survive, would become like Wayne Newton in Vegas, or Sha Na Na at theme parks—that they'd get onstage in the old gear and perform songs from the happy days. The Old School tour would bring them a few much-needed dollars, but I hoped they'd focus on writing new material.

Modern MCs were waving guns, describing the ghetto and cursing on their albums—all in the name of "keeping it real"—but in Whodini's wondrous music, a deeper reality appeared, a reality we could relate to. We all knew the morons and blockheads they described. These dunces were actually the people that we called friends, and we encountered them on a daily basis. In fact, it seemed that most of them were hip-hop's biggest "stars"! For some reason, however, I couldn't get over a growing suspicion that the group would successfully regain their audience, then return to producing the same crap that had alienated their fans the first time around.

"It's 'fun' and it's 'great' and we're 'happy to be back,' but now we got a responsibility to rap music," an adamant Jalil said. He rose from his seat. Behind him, diners wrapped themselves in furs, leathers, gloves, hats and scarves. "We have to make it so people can bring their families and have fun at a rap concert again, you know what I'm saying?"

"People may call us 'legends' and all that but it's good to be humble," Grandmaster Dee smirked, just as the waiter arrived with the check and Jalil stuffed his arms into a bulky leather jacket, bundling up for the storm outside. "We're living legends in the hip-hop world," Jalil conceded, "but the Creator is bigger than all of us. I'm only as big as He wants me to be."

Chapter 11

The Fountain of Youth

■

You sit down to write about an artist and attempt to show why this person is different than the one you wrote about last month. You sit there racking your brain, analyzing transcripts of your conversation, and for the life of you, you can't help but shake your head—realizing that this will be another run-of-the-mill story. At this point, the bottle comes in handy, or yet another pseudonym, which you hide behind out of respect for your supportive readership.

It was a dreary autumn and in the music business money changed hands. The West Coast had their usual suspects releasing shoddy albums, rehashing bromidic themes and fulfilling the prophecy: any radical new voice that sticks around long enough eventually reaches a point where they become the hip-hop equivalent of Earth, Wind & Fire—once heralded as a sparkling new entry, later another money-making entity for the major-label cash-cow system. Time passes and an artist who started with a bang searches for another idea, only to discover that most artists only have one or two things to say in their lifetime, which results in a search for fresh ways to disguise old concepts.

There are many undeserving in the world of hip-hop, many who benefit from full-page ads in music monthlies, who find what was supposed to be a critical media fawning for acceptance, and so it was when Brad Jordan met *The Source* on many occasions. With limited vocabulary and a musical sense that aspired to fatuity, Jordan was nevertheless able to peddle minor contributions into a major career.

Aided and abetted by a compliant media, his music sold, and with the instant success associated with those who did not pay dues, came a certain superiority, an egotism, a refusal to take an objective look at himself and admit that he was lacking in certain vital areas.

Let me tell you about the "gangsta rapper." He (as the most successful are usually male) does not have what it takes to be part of elevating hip-hop. His album sales are high and he enjoys success fast and it does something to him. He looks down his nose at our struggling to reach the level of success and material wealth that was handed to him. But careers built on shock value are short, and when he falls off, looking up at us, this superiority is still just as firm in him as his backbone.

For me to approach Scarface, I must see him from my point of view: if I fall victim to his way of seeing himself, then I'll simply be another hack, another checkbook journalist who flew out to Houston, partied, ignored his album, and returned with platitudes about his generosity, his virtues, his sad rise from the ghetto and, most untrue, his lyrical brilliance. I would be ignoring the fact that he is not, never was, and will probably never be a real MC, and that he has benefited from a mutant variation of hip-hop. I would ignore that each new album from him and his kind makes it harder for true MCs to sign deals, and makes it easier for the poseurs to continue riding high off the hog.

■■

His first sense of superiority came when he was eight years old, after seeing Walter Hill's *The Warriors*, a film about a Brooklyn gang battling their way past rival gangs blocking the way home. Brad Jordan cited that as a major influence, and told a writer about his first gang, a group of kids who called themselves the Panthers. They roamed the streets with "closet sticks" and "beat people's asses, dog," he said.

By thirteen, in junior high, he found another way of gaining attention. He wanted to be "the best break dancer, beat-boxer and rapper.

"I was colder than a motherfucker. I had styles, boy. We was using records, just the intro of somebody's song. We'd be mixing that shit."

Soon after, he entered a group called the Ghetto Boys and under the aegis of Rap-A-Lot Records owner James Smith, fashioned an

Gangsta: Merchandising the Rhymes of Violence

image patterned after NWA. NWA's *Straight Outta Compton* skyrocketed once the press stumbled onto their anti-police attitude. Smith's attitude was, "Gangsta sells," so he encouraged these average inner-city youth, heavy on the brawn, light on the brain, to pen their own sick fantasies.

One of them, the necrophilia described on the song "Mind of a Lunatic," imbued their debut, *Grip It! On That Other Level!*, with a sufficient aura of "controversy," and, like clockwork, the press flocked to the album. After a deal with Rick Rubin's Def American label fell through (which is when they changed their name to "Geto" Boys) Smith released the album on his tiny Rap-A-Lot label and soon found that the negative publicity had, as with NWA, increased interest in the group. With a legion of writers questioning their legitimacy, and various special-interest groups denouncing them, Smith sat back and relaxed. He finally had his own NWA.

Mr. Scarface, the chubby Black guy who scowled in pictures and wore a black Al Capone hat, may not have had the lyrical dexterity of an MC Ren but that was okay. The Geto Boys listener did not want hip-hop. They wanted blood and guts. All Willie D had to do to remain successful was continue to put on that hard face that made him look constipated. NWA may have had Dre's breakbeat-heavy production, endearing them to East Coast traditionalists, and Ice Cube and Ren's stylized deliveries—but did they have Bushwick Bill, the sociopathic elf who idolized Chucky from the *Child's Play* movies and who provided the group with a grotesque visual novelty? No, they didn't, and while Dr. Dre told the media, "I heard of them but I haven't heard their record," labeling them "an NWA take-off," the Geto Boys would continue to bleed the "gangsta" image—and NWA comparisons—for all they were worth.

Since he thrived on the attention of others, Scarface was at home in the Geto Boys, his rough voice and shabby appearance helping listeners see that this group was "telling it like it is." Dazzled by the smoke and mirrors, the average Geto Boys fan would not read between the lines, would not be jolted by Bushwick Bill admitting that their inspiration came from "watching stuff like *Robocop* and *Terminator* and Freddie and Jason, you know what I'm sayin'?" or from neighborhood gossip: "—about a girl gettin' killed, and all they found was her head and her arm, and a leg, you know. They started finding the

The Fountain of Youth

body piece by piece, and there was a whole big search on TV and everything." They wouldn't care that this was all a fantasy.

■■■

Scarface and I first spoke after his involvement in a gunfight. After a performance in Shreveport, Louisiana, he entered a restaurant and encountered "gangbangers," he explained. An argument became a fight, then a shootout and then, after a police officer became involved, a tragedy. His best friend, Rudy, he called him, was shot and left to die.

He was indignant that this could happen, that his friend could actually die in such a senseless, unexpected manner, that he felt "911 was a joke," and that the police somehow wanted his friend to die, and he said so.

This was around the time when Willie D grew resentful and left the group, intent on releasing a solo album that would "redefine the meaning of rap." While *I'm Going Out Like a Soldier* was a commercial failure, it did get press coverage with a provocatively titled song, "Fuck Rodney King," which Willie, on hard times indeed, promoted by standing near coffins at the 1992 Republican National Convention.

When Bushwick Bill got drunk one night, he pulled a gun and demanded that his girlfriend kill him. If she didn't, he would kill her infant. He kneeled before her and started to hand her the weapon; she tried to grab it—to prevent him from hurting himself since he was drunk—and *POW!* One of his eyes was shot out.

The group was in a state of dissipation, in the grip of a madness that usually strikes the poor who have suddenly been handed large amounts of money and success. They struggled to get out of the ghetto and found that to stay out they would continually have to be near it at all times.

In keeping with the group's exploitative tradition, group members visited Bill at hospital with a cameraman, propped Bill up in a wheelchair and posed alongside his chair as if he were Professor X and they were his trusty mutant sidekicks. This was the ultimate grotesquerie, the lowest hip-hop artists have ever stooped. Bill looked as if he had barely left the operating room, still wearing a patient's gown with a huge wad of gauze over the damaged socket, and his bandmates were

Gangsta: Merchandising the Rhymes of Violence

smiling, as if contemplating the many album sales this latest "controversy" would generate. As if this moment of drunken stupidity would serve as a testament to their standing as ghetto ambassadors.

"Motherfuckers wanna make some money I guess," Dr. Dre had said earlier, and this motivation had reached nightmarish proportions. In their videos during this confused phase Bill would reach into his face and pluck out his prosthetic eye, plopping it into glasses of water as if to show the viewer that the loss of an eye was a small thing indeed when compared to maintaining a career. The permanent loss of an eye was not a handicap, he seemed to say: it was simply another visual gimmick, which the group needed badly, as they they had seemingly peaked with their single, "My Mind's Playing Tricks on Me."

During these troubling days, Scarface avoided the public eye. The gunfight seemed to be enough to center him. He disappeared until it was time to promote his next solo album, when he once again became a familiar face on video channels, standing near gravesites or overseeing funerals, mouthing veiled lyrics about his friend Rudy's death over dirgelike melodies. In interviews promoting the new solo album, he downplayed the death, clarified that he was not pursuing a case against the police department—it was ultimately up to Rudy's family—and added that he was now dating a police officer.

We spoke again, over the phone in December 1994, and he admitted that the status of the Geto Boys was a mystery. "Hopefully, we'll all get back together, man, but you know, until then I'm solo," he said, again promoting solo work. "I don't know how they gonna handle it," he added, as if a millions of miles away from them. "I'm in it for the business. Geto Boys is a business now. I really can't touch on it 'cause I don't know what's in the works for the group. I'd like to do another album but you know—that's just life." But there would definitely be another album, he emphasized. He simply didn't know when. "But there'll be one, though. I may not even be a member but they'll do another one for sure."

IV

By late 1994, the heat was on gangsta rap, with Congress holding hearings on the music and trying to determine if it was indeed harmful to the children. And yet, G-funk—"gangsta rap" set to Parlia-

Funkadelicized grooves—was selling more than ever.

After *The Chronic* album, Dr. Dre produced Snoop Doggy Dogg's 4,000,000-selling *DoggyStyle* and completed his transformation from malevolent woman-beater to mellow convertible-driving pothead. As with his NWA work, producers scurried to throw together sound-alikes, to find studios that had Moog keyboards on the premises and to find MCs capable of scrawling their own Snoop-like lyrics, capable of fusing the gangsta machismo of NWA to Slick Rick's comedic storytelling:

Kris Kross producer Jermaine Dupri released a female Snoop (Da Brat, whose lackluster *Funkdafied* sold a million copies); MC Hammer, working with the Dogg Pound, returned sans diaper pants and became the world's first singing-and-dancing gangsta; Dana Dane modified his own Slick Rick imitation; Gang Starr laid synths on *Hard to Earn*; Naughty By Nature hooked up with Road Dawgs, a group of Bloods from Inglewood; Queen Latifah's *Black Reign* revealed a Snoop influence; Ill Al Skratch's "Where's My Homies" earned them their fifteen minutes; R. Kelly became the G-funk lover-man and, most surprisingly, Slick Rick teamed him with Warren G.

And now, Scarface arrived with his own exploitation of funk's nostalgia value, his own sweet melodies that would further guarantee gangsta rap's survival.

"You doing alright?" Scarface asked, prepared to promote his latest album, a G-funk work called *The Diary*. I said yes and asked about the change in direction, from middling breakbeats to polished production.

"I was always musically inclined growing up," he said proudly. "Any instrument you can name, I can play." He cited Marley Marl, Dr. Dre and Geroge Clinton as influences, then, with a trace of condescension, threw in a high-brow nod to Pink Floyd's Roger Waters and David Gilmore. For lyrics, his inspiration, surprisingly, came from East Coast mainstays Rakim, the Blastmaster KRS-One and Kool G Rap. He just loved them, he said. "But that doesn't necessarily reflect on my style. That's who I like. That's who I listen to."

His voice became distant, the telephone receiver away from his mouth. "Double X," I heard him say.

"And the Double X Posse?"

"What?! Oh no, no, man. I'm just in this store buying something. . . ."

When I conveyed the general opinion, that his singsong flow on the single "I Seen a Man Cry" evoked comparisons to Buckshot Shorty of Black Moon, he said, "Who the fuck is Buckshot Shorty?! He from New York?!"

▼

The Source had been kind to Scarface. A few months ago, there he was sitting in a low-rider with MC Eiht and Spice One, sitting in on something called a "Gangsta Rap Summit." Here he was now with his own cover, with no story to go along with it a few hours before deadline, revealing that he was your average MC, no different than any other gangsta, save for the fact that his songs usually found him shot, buried or insane.

The formula had proved effective enough to cause his solo albums, *Mr. Scarface Is Back* and *The World Is Yours*, to sell over 500,000 copies each, and it was capable of holding his audience close to him, even as he strayed from his basics and delved into a more emotional brand of blood-and-guts. "That's how it go," he explained, as if to a five-year-old who refuses to listen.

"That's real life," was the reason his lyrics never ventured into anything more substantial — "the 'one day you're here, the next day you're gone' type . . . coming in, going out . . . You're coming in killing, you're going out killed—"

It was amusing: Scarface and his ilk sensed that the public was tired of the recurring motifs in gangsta rap and yet they would not, or could not, change. Some raised a stink about the most basic political issues but could not resist the compulsion to revert to type: eventually they offered disquisitions on guzzling 40s, selling drugs and shooting people. Under the pretense of "street reporting" they negated anything positive they may have had to offer.

Scarface could pose, posture, huff and puff about "reality" and reveal a philosophical view of death, but he couldn't escape the fact that gangsta rappers were the latest sellouts to betray their principals or espoused causes for royalty checks and MTV airplay. He quoted the Charles Barkley party line and said he didn't want to be a role model, which was admirable in this case due to the image he promoted, but ultimately a cop-out.

"I like for little kids to look at me and say, 'Yeah man, that nigga 'Face is getting his scratch on, that's his hustle,' " he said. "But the little kids don't necessarily have to, you know, follow in my footsteps. I want them to look at me and say, 'Yeah, man, he getting his hustle on, I'm fittin' to get mine too.' I don't want a motherfucker to be like, 'Aw, I wanna be just like him when I grow up.' That ain't me, man."

The whole marketing strategy behind gangsta rap was that the rappers were street reporters, even though residents of the ghettos name-dropped on wax found fault with the music. Drug-related murders did occur and police did harass Blacks, but not on the consistent basis described on wax.

How could artists like Scarface speak of killing up to thirty people on one song, then claim to be speaking reality? "If you're a gangsta, then what are you doing in show business?" KRS-One, one of Scarface's favorites, inquired. How can describing the madness, without offering possible solutions or any helpful information, help matters any?

"Well, how can the news help matters any?" he demanded. "How can anything help matters get better? That's their 'hustle.' Their rapping is their hustle. My rapping is my 'hustle.' I ain't say I was no preacher or no reverend or no prophet. I said I was an entertainer, man, and I'm doing entertainment. Like I say, Ted Koppel or whoever the fuck they is, or Donahue or— Them motherfuckers ain't making shit better! I'm reporting, they reporting. I can't knock their hustle. You a journalist. You're writing this story. That's your hustle."

"What would you say to this comment?" I said. " 'Gangsta rap is hyped up by large corporations that are exploiting a trend', that 'the music reinforces negative stereotypes about Black people'?"

"What's 'negative stereotypes about Black people'? This real shit that's going on? Is that what it is? I don't understand the question. Bring it to me again."

"Okay. 'Gangsta rap is hyped up by large corporations . . .' "

"Like record companies?" he obstructed.

"Yeah. 'The music reinforces negative stereotypes about Black people.' "

"Dude. Dude. Dude," he said, his voice louder each time. "Look

Gangsta: Merchandising the Rhymes of Violence

at Black people and answer that question yourself. Just print that. Tell them to look at Black people. Just look at them." He was on the ropes, struggling to regain his footing. "Man, I'll tell you what. It ain't my fault. And I don't understand that record company— You're saying that record companies are blowing this shit up to make Black people look bad, right?"

"No, that record companies are pushing this type of rap to make money."

"To me, Black folk make Black folk look bad," he said, the foot digging deeper into his mouth, "and we been doing that shit for hundreds of years. We been making each other look bad. The record companies ain't got shit to do with that. The news makes people look bad; shit, magazines make niggas look bad; niggas make niggas look bad. It ain't they fault that niggas look bad."

"If you could change one thing about all of gangsta rap, what would it be and why?"

"I wouldn't wanna change shit. I'd change the way people look at it. Instead of being so one-sided about it, they should be more open-minded to this real shit that's really going on. 'Cause it is really going on. I ain't saying no shit that ain't never gonna happen in a million years. I ain't talking about no *Demolition Man*– or *Nightmare on Elm Street*–type shit! But they love that! I ain't talking about no *Terminator 2* but they into that!

"They just fucking with niggas cause niggas is getting paid doing this shit. So that's what the 'big issue' is! And niggas always been against niggas! So if I'm doing better than this nigga, then this nigga's gonna try to knock me! So niggas is against niggas as well the white folk! Rap is catching it from both sides. As long as you're kissing ass"—sonorously—" 'You gonna be alright,' but the minute you start speaking out about the real shit? Motherfuckers are gonna start 'disliking' you."

He had written about sex with a corpse in a graphic manner. "That's my point!" he interrupted. "I'm like a narrator, a movie director like Spielberg." Not Spielberg; more like *Phantasm*, *The Wall*, *Boyz N the Hood*, *Menace II Society*, *Jason's Lyric* and his other favorites. And *Natural Born Killers*, where the media turned psychopaths into folk heroes, which he hadn't seen yet.

"Talking won't make that shit better," he finally acknowledged.

"You got motherfuckers that's been talking about it for years and they ain't did shit. And I would name off some names but I'd be wrong." The only controversy surrounding gangsta rap was that "it's a bunch of motherfuckers who's talking about it but ain't doing shit," he admitted.

VI

"Well, shit. I ain't trying to make things better," he continued. "That's not me. I'm just talking about it. The motherfucking news ain't trying to make shit better. What the fuck they doing to make shit better? Fuck that. That ain't my responsibility."

His voice grew distant again, cloudy, as if someone had placed a thick towel over the receiver. "Well, if it don't fit I'm just gonna bring it back," I heard him tell a salesperson at the store.

"Hello?" he said. "I'm sorry."

It was no problem; I simply had one or two final questions since I knew he was busy.

"Oh, I ain't . . . I ain't in no rush, man, I got all day."

"Okay, we were discussing . . . You said that it's not your responsibility . . ."

"I don't want these," he told the salesperson. "I changed my mind. [*To me*] Go 'head, I'm listening."

I could imagine a salesgirl staring at this hip-hop celebrity, shaking her head and thinking, "They are different from you and me." He had been in the store for close to thirty minutes, on their phone long-distance, selecting merchandise, sending it back for proper-size items, then saying he would not be buying anything.

I asked about his five-year-old son, about what it was like to have Scarface as a daddy and heard his voice brighten.

"Shit. My kids get anything they want but I ain't Daddy at this time of the year 'cause I'm hella busy." His voice grew portentous. "I can say this. This may be, I don't know, but this may be my last two years in this shit. I might do another album, maybe another Geto Boys album and a solo and that's gonna be it for me, man.

"I'm gonna retire, man," he continued, sounding as if the fountain of youth had dried up, as if hanging with the rowdy hooligans in hip-hop was no longer enough to repel encroaching adult responsibility. "I don't know. I'm getting old." The concept of viewing one-

self as old at the age of twenty-three may sound abnormal to someone who has not lived what can be kindly described as a full life, but
I understood. This industry was full of shit and he wanted to get out
now before it chewed him up and spit him out. He was like Kurtz in
that cave, rubbing his forehead, considering what he'd been through,
calling it "the horror, the horror."

"I been in this motherfucker for close to eight years. Two more
years and that's retirement. That'll be ten years. I'm going out like Jordan, too. Everybody's gonna say, 'Aw, he coming back, he coming
back.' " He just wanted to rest, he was exhausted from the touring and
situations on the road. "Shit, I just wanna sit my fat ass down. For real."
He feigned a laugh then yawned. "I'm tired as a motherfucker."

"What else are you up to?"

"Shit, I ain't really up to nothing. Finding myself now."

His fans imagined that "Mr. Scarface" spent his time in shoot-outs
and car chases, but his average day was more sedate. "I'll be out there
hanging out with my brother, getting bored, hanging out with my
potna, getting bored, you know, and going home at the end of the
night . . . make it home at like eleven-thirty 'cause I don't be doing
no lot of hanging out no more. I got old! I'm telling you: I got old!"

The "Tony Montana" image he cultivated was a sham. There were
no thrones set up in business offices; no huge mansions with high
gates and guard dogs; no piles of cocaine; no stacks of drug money;
no triple-beam scales or M-16s. Just a twenty-three-year-old young father who kept repeating, "I got old! I'm telling you: I got old!"

I asked if anything had happened to him to bring this on.

"Yeah," he answered, sounding more than a little eccentric. "The
rappers just coming in be saying like, 'Damn, I used to listen to you,
man. I came up on you man!'

"I feel old," he said again, trying to convince himself more than
anything, as if feeling old would keep him out of trouble and alive.
"I'm outdated now." If he wanted to feel old at twenty-three and that
he should retire when his new album was receiving good reviews and
a strong push from a major label, that was his prerogative. Being artistic led one into strange new terrain. Instead of offering advice, I asked
what he would say to newer acts.

"Watch the record business," he said instantly. "It's what Tribe
Called Quest talk about. The record-company people are shady like

a motherfucker. Shady, shady, shady! You got to watch them. And when you're touring, it's cool to be down, but don't be no goddamned fool, going to other cities and fucking shit up for the people who gotta tour! There's so much shit that goes on on the road." He mentioned how, for a minute, his group was banned from California by hostile audiences, then said, "It ain't just Tupac or Snoop. It ain't just them that's out there. Little bitty groups fuck it up for when the big people come in."

In two years, he admitted, he hoped to be like Dr. Dre at Death Row or Russell Simmons at Rush: behind a desk at his label Face-2-Face, running a musical empire, advising newer groups to be more like Snoop Doggy Dogg, or better yet, NWA, since "gangsta sells"; helping these newjacks benefit from his experience as someone who once had to perform gangsta raps on stage every night.

As he spoke about his future, Oliver Stone's screenplay for *Scarface* came to mind. Brad Jordan, older, wiser and heavier — in photos he frequently held 40s of malt liquor — would abandon his childish past and focus on big business. But instead of his cinematic idol's M-60 and goon squad, the maleficent "Bad Guy" would use new groups to cut into his rivals' profits. This small label, like Rap-A-Lot he hoped, would force the competition to be attentive, and when this was done, Scarface's many years of railing against the system would pay off. The whiteys he dissed would shake his hand, take him to dinner, accept his phone calls. For now, like so many other twenty-somethings in the 1990s, he felt depleted, more than a little lost. "I been around, man," he said again. "I'm tired and I'm'a take a rest."

The Fresh New Face on the Scene

■

When a new artist sees his album released in stores, he acts in a very peculiar manner. Now that Method Man had a record contract of his own, everyone wanted to shake his hand, but he still he felt that people were trying to manipulate him. Why would the former societal outsider suddenly be the center of their attention? Everyone had a kind word to say about him and the labels on Sixth Avenue that would never have given him the time of day now considered him the band to beat.

He had a contract and a label paying him and adequate promotional backing; he attended parties in fashionable hot spots; he smoked the choicest weeds and held his composure when celebrities he once admired from afar crossed rooms to introduce themselves. R&B singers and West Coast gangsta rappers invited him to appear on remixes, and paid him for his time. He hoped that his erratic style would stray from the formulaic drivel glutting the market and inspire derisive ostracism from his peers and critics; but his style was quickly accepted to the point of actually bridging even the long-standing coastal rivalries. Instant success had indeed arrived, and for Meth the word *traveling* no longer evoked images of sailing into Lower Manhattan on the Staten Island Ferry.

It was a rainy gray January afternoon and Meth was sitting in Def Jam's offices. Interviewers from magazines he used to religiously follow would tape, transcribe and print his every opinion. He was the fresh new face on the scene who could do no wrong. Everyone wanted to claim him as part of their circle.

Def Jam Records had pressured him into adding a distinct chorus to each of his songs but the album still carried his personal imprint. After success with the Wu-Tang Clan, Def Jam, ever seeking to exploit a trend, promptly signed him. They were treating Meth very nicely, like everyone else, and Meth — basking in the attention — mistook their financial interest for actual concern.

He sat behind a desk, high as hell — Fitzgerald would've wrote he was "tight" — and stared at the flickering images on a small color television set. He was on the tail end of a bender, a one-man party that started in Japan and was kept alive by the need to escape his suddenly busy schedule.

"We were getting buck naked onstage, all that shit, man," he said of Japan. The groupies had worked their magic on him and he was sad to leave but there was a video to film in Miami, Florida. He was developing slight laryngitis but couldn't have canceled his engagements if he wanted to. They were too important. After the video shoot and subsequent partying, he boarded a flight to North Carolina, where he bonded with Biggie Smalls and performed at a concert. A fight broke out in the audience and he was elated; he would be able to rest and wouldn't have to lifelessly perform his entire album.

Hours later, he flew to the next stop on his itinerary: a performance at Washington, D.C.'s Howard University. His schedule was as busy as those described in many Hendrix biographies. "I was tired as a motherfucker, smoking mad weed, not eating, all that shit," Meth said, proud for some reason. After the show, he boarded a plane heading right back to Miami, Florida, and attended a music-industry convention. Between parties and panels, he found time to don his heavy black leather coat and hiking boots to do some water-skiing.

"I'm in Florida now," he slowly clarified, his eyes brimming with exhaustion. "I didn't go to sleep. I'm just charged. I didn't know where this extra energy was coming from." He performed at a nightclub and returned to his hotel where he got high with local MCs waiting out front. "I was out there with them till daylight almost before I went upstairs. I ain't get no sleep."

A mild psychosis settled over him. He was now visibly exhausted and as wired as a speed freak. Speaking as quickly as he had on his

Gangsta: Merchandising the Rhymes of Violence

album, he spit out phrases as disjointed as any by Burroughs. His brain was sharp, his senses altered by insomnia; each phrase or uncompleted thought held private meaning; frequently he laughed. His eyes were big as saucers, his teeth covered with fang-shaped gold caps. Given the context, a hip-hop interview, he was amusing; anywhere else, people would begin to move away from him.

He watched a video, moving hands or knees or both, unable to keep still, his body a ball of energy. Two brats were onscreen, with jeans hanging off their asses and bouncing to a funk track. They wore Big Boots like everyone else but accessorized with alternative nose rings. Meth liked this group Quo; they were nothing but a salt-and-pepper Kris Kross clone but he liked them. He shrieked, pointing a bony finger at the white dwarf and yelling, "That motherfucker can dance!

"Usually white kids can't," he said in a hushed tone.

His eyes were as transfixed as a witch staring into a crystal ball, but his hands impulsively rolled a cigar. The first pull was a long one and filled the room with a diabolically seductive aroma. He was surrounded by smoke. The Quo video faded out and a commercial began advertising Meth's own "Bring the Pain." It was coming soon to The Box, the television promised.

Meth stared at the screen as if he were watching an evil stranger. He was reliving the adventure, and accepting that the starmaking process had officially begun. First he was shown hijacking a city bus, then after an edit, he sat in the rear with shabby potheads and drunks. Then he marched through a crowded red-lit basement party in a trendy vest, sagging jeans and boots as awkward looking as those worn by Quo a minute ago.

The commercial ended and, satisfied, Meth boasted of how the usually unyielding Def Jam executives allowed him creative input on the planning of his video. An aspiring director, he pointed at the screen and proudly took credit for the achromatic zombie eyes he flashed at the camera. Waving the 40-ounce beer and partying with rowdy thugs in a secret hangout were also his concepts.

He sat behind the desk in an office he had commandeered from a Def Jam publicist and restrained himself from cheering when he saw himself onscreen, releasing ribbons of marijuana smoke from his mouth.

" 'What the Bloodclot' is gonna be the shit when that come out," he predicted, as excited as a kid opening gifts on Christmas. "That's gonna be my fourth video," he said, savvy enough to realize that you were only as good as your last song. "And they better give me four mics and not try to pull no shit," he said of *The Source*, " 'cause I'll have every motherfucker I know up in there committing every crime known to man." He turned away from the television and fixed us with an uncharacteristic squint. "I ain't fucking around."

■■

> " 'You want it all?' (Yeah) I want it all like that! /
> I'll stab my own moms in the back for a stack!"
> —Method Man, "I Get My Thang in Action"

The Def Jam publicist returned to his office and said he needed to make a few phone calls so Meth rose from the man's chair, wiped away some ashes he had flicked on the desk and walked out. The well-dressed females working in the office stopped and giggled when they saw the bushy-haired new rebel. He smiled coyly, feigned ignorance, looked this way and that as if seeking guidance then stomped down a corridor.

Everyone greeted him pleasantly, shook his hand and did their best to make him feel at home but when he turned his back they scowled. He was the humble star smiling graciously and they were his in-evitable critics.

The conference room was empty so he walked towards another television set. Someone pulled out a pack of cigarettes, a brand called Beadies, and Meth sat up as quickly as a moviegoer who discovers that a boring film had suddenly grown exciting. "Oh! You got Beadies?!" he asked, exasperated. "Can I get one? I don't care: I'll even pay you for the shit!" The Beadie smoker was an ardent fan and would have gladly handed over the entire pack. And Meth knew it. We sat in silence, half watching cartoons until Bönz Malone arrived half-drunk and an hour late.

Bönz had been an instant sensation when he first appeared in national magazines. He knew everyone in the industry and everyone was proud to know him. In that way, he was like Meth. They were both

Gangsta: Merchandising the Rhymes of Violence

well-loved eccentrics and they were both amazed that everyone would pay serious money for their humorous ramblings.

Bönz always reminded me of Perry White from the *Superman* comic books. On the surface, he was a hard-boiled, demanding type who spoke in well-loved clichés and was always—even now, almost a decade after his arrival—the life of the party. The casual observer could never suspect that he harbored quixotic notions on American journalism, moral fiber and professional objectivity. In private, with that rare friend or two that he trusted, he would discuss mobster films, music that struck him as particularly sad or the latest book he'd read before beginning to analyze the dynamics of his own troubled life. He had become well-respected in his field and broken many barriers, but he had also become the subject of repeated rumors about his drinking.

After he removed the jacket he'd been drinking in for three nights, Bönz bummed a Newport and set his Dictaphone on the table. He sat in a chair directly across from Method, an old friend and smoking partner, played with a lighter, then lit his cigarette and smiled as Meth held his own Beadie at arm's length and complimented its taste.

Meth compulsively inhaled and his ardent fan, a blossoming five-percenter, tried to imitate him. Newports were maligned as a "white man's poison" by hip-hop's more extreme elements but Bönz actually seemed to enjoy the cigarette even more. I lit one myself, and remembered what Zev Love X once told me. "Tell Black people to stop fucking with those Newports," he warned while puffing on a Newport. "They're killing us up."

After stubbing out the Beadie, Meth gnawed into a chicken sandwich that a female publicist had left on the table. He answered a few of Bönz's offbeat questions. During a lull in the conversation, Meth's gaze again strayed towards the television screen, towards a commercial for the latest Batman action figure.

"Bob Kane's gettin' all that money," Meth muttered.

We had been in the room for over an hour and the "serious" interview between veteran Bönz and newcomer Method had deteriorated into a struggle between court jesters. They were engrossing, amusing, like Boris Karloff and Vincent Price as sorcerers in *The Raven.*

I glanced at the television and tried watching the beginning of a Japanese live-action program, another with colorful superheroes, a computerized mentor, a talking animal and monstrous creatures from outer space. One of these shows was no different than another and it didn't matter which was which.

"That shit right there's better than *Power Rangers*!" Meth said, attracted by its flashy rock-music theme. "VR Troopers, they get down!"

"This is *Super Samurai Cyber Squad,*" I corrected.

"That's the industry right there." He leaned towards Bönz across the table.

"*Mighty Morphin Power Rangers* got paid out the ass, now they got *Super Samurai Squad* and *VR Troopers*! 'Where *Mighty Morphin Power Rangers* left off!'" he bellowed.

"That's what I'm talking about!" he said, his blood boiling. "A rap star fall into that shit, you could just hang it up. We get sidetracked when some new fad comes out. Like when that 'club era' came out, then there's like a new 'reggae era.'" The hip-hop audience were sheep who blindly followed trends, Meth opined, holding court for hours, smoking cigars and imparting pearls of wisdom hard-learned. His career was taking off and he felt the love of everyone around him: he could do no wrong; he was the fresh new face in the crowd.

Bönz's eyes were glowing and he was genuinely happy for Meth — he deserved his success — but Bönz knew this industry too well. After a while, Meth sat quietly and chain-smoked. In Meth's youthful bluster, he saw himself years ago, as he was when he first made his mark and everyone rushed to do as he did and suddenly, consciously misspelling words became all the rave. It was good that Meth would have some early happiness, Bönz nodded to himself. It would help him through the hard times.

Superpimp Meets the Real World

■

"The city is up and coming, and they say in a few years when they have finally established themselves, motherfuckers are gonna want to get in and it's gonna cost you."

—Too $hort

It was a prematurely cold, black autumn evening in November 1994 and the sidewalks were littered with crisp brown leaves, broken tree branches and wine bottles. Atlanta's International Boulevard was ghostly silent and devoid of the rhythm you'd find in any other major American city. There was hardly any traffic, and no loud music filtered out of nightclubs or bars. I strolled towards a liquor store, to buy another 40, and noticed that white police cruisers—with caged rear windows for boisterous offenders—were slowing to a crawl at the sight of me. I was a strange face, and wearing a heavy black wool knit cap; there was no telling what I was up to.

Atlanta was far from an elysian field. A serial killer had been apprehended tonight. A thin white man who slaughtered a local homosexual on Mother's Day before roaming to other states to continue his twenty-victim massacre. There had also been three slayings in the last month near the Morehouse campus. Another maniac tried to abduct a female Christmas shopper from the parking lot of a mall.

After grabbing her neck, he tried, unsuccessfully, to yank her into his van.

The air was frosty but the mob of panhandling crack addicts didn't seem to notice. Ghastly and ghostly, they were in need of that next hit. I watched them shamble through darkness like zombies in a graveyard. The war on drugs had obviously failed in Atlanta as well, and for some reason, I pictured Pablo Escobar laughing in his grave.

"They try to say everything's alright but this is still a white man's town," said Mack, a homeless Black man in his thirties who accompanied me to another deli (the liquor store was closed). "I used to work at this parking lot, managing the shit and making money for the owners, but then these crackers tried to railroad me out of there!"

We marched over a bridge, through barren streets, and Mack pointed to the nearby CNN tower, sanguinary letters aglow in neon. Ted Turner was a prosperous redneck who joked about his loyal Black gardener in *Jet* magazine, a yokel who tried to attach himself to the beautiful people by marrying Jane Fonda (once called "Hanoi Jane" for supporting America's enemies in Vietnam). "I try to tell younger cats that all of this was built on the Black man's blood but they don't listen," Mack whined. "Ted Turner never had no money for no TV station! Unless it was from his family, and his family may have owned slaves back then!"

The Ku Klux Klan had abandoned their nocturnal hooded hijinks for three-piece suits and corporate day jobs; steeds were replaced by new-model Ford trucks. And about Atlanta (population 425,022) being a "big money" sector? He scoffed. Tell that to the crackheads who leaped out of bushes with outstretched palms or the killers near the Black campus; to the budding hate groups—comprised of unemployed whites—in neighboring counties or to the vicious small-town sheriffs who still thought it was 1950. It was a mystery why many Blacks were returning to this racially divided "New South," Mack admitted. They would soon learn, he warned.

■■

After arriving at three that afternoon, I had stepped out of the airport with my bag—traveling light as usual and with a slight hangover. The sun beat down on my back like a whip; everything looked the brightest yellow. An elevated subway could take me downtown for a dollar but I jumped into a cab. The driver, a Haitian man with nervous eyes, asked if he could play music. "Sure," I answered, if I could light a cigarette. He gave me the old "secondhand smoke" routine. These anti-smoking laws were complicating life.

An odious Heavy D rap scratched out of crackly speakers. Why was it that artists who couldn't get arrested in New York always seemed to be immensely popular in rural areas?

We turned onto a highway congested with traffic. White people in pickup trucks and hatchbacks honked at Blacks in old-model Cadillacs and Fords. The downtown skyline lay ahead of us like a promised land, visible no matter how the road curved.

Uncompleted stadiums—part of Atlanta's "new" image—stood across from battered old civil-rights churches. The driver kept rewinding Heavy D's "Black Coffee, No Sugar, No Cream" (or whatever it was called) as we passed poor Black women with children at a bus stop. One yelled at her child to "get over here"; the woman's T-shirt had gone to seed, her hair was on end and her cheekbones looked sunken. There were tall bland buildings, a cluster of modern brick-and-glass structures housing the police department, city hall and the courthouse, and unfinished construction sites with skeletal girders, ropes, piles of dirt and cement mixers. Black cops in light brown shirts stood in front of the entrance to a building or mounted bulky motorcycles.

As the dusty cab approached the chaste Omni Hotel, decrepit two-story houses were replaced by modern business towers and banks. But gentrification had not overwhelmed those who owned the area's "rib shacks." These Black businessmen were here long before the "New South" was ever planned, and they'd keep their shabby little establishments right here amid the newer, glittering office towers until yuppies on their lunch hours no longer brought their business. There were impressive, formidable corporate headquarters but there were also reminders that all was not well with people like those who loitered in front of the Checks Cashed, liquor store or barbershop.

The city was "being rebuilt" in time for the upcoming Olympics— former President Jimmy Carter's organization had their hammers and nails out—but many whites still expected Blacks to end sentences with "sir" and "ma'am." In the Omni lobby, beer-bellied white men pulled their white women close. It was as if I were covered in blood, as if my animal lust would compel me to rape and ravage their porcelain trophies.

■■■

Since 1980, while in high school, Oakland rapper Too $hort had been turning immature sex raps into large royalty checks. A shrewd businessman even at fifteen, he appeared at whatever party he could find, wearing a monogrammed jacket and peddling tapes. After he opened for UTFO (he told S. H. Fernando that, without a record, "here was 7,500 people singing with me word for word"), he teamed with a local drug dealer, who gave him money, a car and access to a studio.

His reputation and large sales figures inspired Jive/RCA to sign him in early 1988, and by age twenty-six, he had seen his first album sell 500,000 copies, and albums number two and three sell over a million each. His formula was clearly defined, advantageous and recognizable so, to appease him, Jive signed his producer Ant Banks and whoever else he brought their way (as they'd done for Jazzy Jeff's colleagues when Jeff's records sold).

$hort would cruise through the sunny streets of Oakland in new cars, hobnob with celebrities and fans, flaunt chunky jewels, spend money and live a lifestyle learned from *Superfly* and *The Mack*. He resided in a large home and owned a production/management company called Dangerous Music. By tackling as many jobs as he could—producing, manufacturing, marketing and promoting, he was able to turn "a handsome profit," as Reginald Dennis once wrote, flaunting the fact that $hort had once sold "15,000 tapes in seven days and pocketed 60 Gs."

In 1995, his seventh album, *Cocktales*, sent cryptic messages to his label. He wanted a million dollars or he'd be retiring. "I actually don't want a million," he readily admitted. "I'm just trying to tell them that they need to pay the artists more fairly." His impending retirement would actually be a search for a label that would pay "Michael Jackson–type money."

I'd been sent to Atlanta because he'd recently moved there, and locals were already complaining about his conduct in downtown strip clubs. He'd drink bubbly and yell lewd comments at the ladies.

"The whole move to Atlanta was about money," he confessed. "In 1993, Dangerous Music was outgrowing its location in Oakland, which was a three-bedroom home. We started getting up to our necks in equipment, boxes of shit just laying around, old records, you name it."

Another motivation was revealed by Spice One: $hort had been "chased out of town," he said. "They trying to *kill* niggas like me and $hort over stupid shit."

"See, Oakland's not as big as Los Angeles," $hort continued. "It's not like you'll get in some shit then not see someone for a while. In Oakland, you'll always see them: rolling in their car, walking down the street, in a store . . . I saw the way things were getting and started thinking: What day will it be that they get me?" He imagined a scenario: he'd walk into a liquor store and a demented fan "would be like, 'Hey, Too $hort!'" before opening fire.

So here he was in the "New Black Music" mecca, Sports-car City, (actually a big country-western town with little rap to be found on the FM band), land of uncompleted stadiums, southern whites, cautious Blacks, and music moguls Jermaine Dupri and Dallas Austin. "And the Black colleges!" $hort yelled, as if he were a member of the city's tourism board.

"Atlanta's like a meeting place for young Black people," he mechanically added. "We're in demand! It's cool to drive a Benz and be a young brother. The police don't try to pull you over and ask you to step out of the car. Some of the cops out here are even Too $hort fans!" According to $hort, the days of local sheriffs collaborating with the Klan, as they had in the sixties, seventies, and eighties, had ended. Today, you could see Black officers walking the streets, cruising in squad cars or riding on motorcycles.

Terence was a friend of a friend and he had taken a day off from his job at a Red Lobster. The pay was decent but he had to kiss ass; he felt uncomfortable calling people "sir" and "ma'am." He was a $hort fan, and hoped to meet his idol, so he was eager to drive me around. After stopping at a small barbershop for a trim and seeing elderly men argue over who was the true "shoeshine king," I asked Terence to stop at a store. It was early morning but I needed my second 40 of the day. He listened to Nate Dogg's dreary, fatalistic "One More Day." He stopped at a red light, near a large subway terminal, in a busier section of town. Shady characters guarded liquor stores, students with books under their arms scurried through the heavy traffic.

Three kids in a smoke-breathing jalopy pulled up on the passenger's side; they coldly eyed Terence. He must have been listening to too much Nate Dogg. He said he regretted not bringing his "strap" with him. "You need it for this part," he said, as if the "New South" were gang-plagued California.

IV

$hort sat on a wooden stool of the type once used in public schools for disciplining a dunce. He put on his friendliest smile and faced a video camera. He had many plans for Dangerous Music, he told the host of Clark University's video show. It would also be the name of the new studio opening soon in "Oakland, Georgia," he laughed. Members of his crew—who resembled children in their parents' clothing, or extras on *Good Times*—listened, nodding when their names were called.

"So how'd you come to Atlanta?" the host sniveled.

"I moved down here after the Freaknik," he answered. An annual gathering of college students and aroused locals, the Freaknik was a weekend of debauchery, perversion, loud music and drug use; it was an overpublicized Roman orgy set to hip-hop and R&B. He had enjoyed himself so much, he stayed an extra two weeks, $hort explained. A friend knew he was about to buy a home in Oakland but sold him on Georgia's virtues. "How much you willing to spend?" he was asked.

"Oh, about $400,000—"

"And you get to live like a king in Atlanta, right," the host demanded, trying his best to fuel the hype. The region was pathologically obsessed with its own reflection and it was difficult to find a billboard that didn't read GEORGIA ON MY MIND.

$hort's minions fiddled with their bass guitars and keyboards. He kept his strained eyes on me. He had probably heard about my rampage before leaving New York. I'd had a bit too much to drink and visited his label Jive's offices: I met his publicist, a whiny little kiss-ass, and tried to tell her my opinion of her artist. But she kept yapping and didn't let me get a word in edgewise, so I finally shouted that he was wack! Another employee, a tall male intern, tried to rush to her rescue but was told that his head was about to be shoved through a car windshield. I wasn't proud of these antics; I had a lot to be angry about back then. It would be Thanksgiving soon, I was an alcoholic and holidays were always extremely difficult.

I was in Atlanta now; it was mid-morning; I was half-drunk and I'd somehow gotten a haircut.

"We're gonna go into the video for 'C.R.E.A.M' by the Wu-Tang Clan!" said the host. $hort rose from his seat. "I'm out of here," he said disgustedly. This, coming from a "rapper" who proudly bragged, "We ain't doing no freestyles, don't even know how to do that shit."

The media were to blame; the writers created this monster. Their ten-dollar words concealed that his rhyming skills were limited. They focused on anything under the sun. His "pimp" image was more intriguing. "I know real pimps and they'll tell me shit that happens," he told *4080*. He had feelings for his mother: "She's been to a few concerts, and I get really uncomfortable when I know my mother's in the crowd," he told *Vibe*. Behind the mack image lurked a business-minded young chap. ("By the time I went nationwide, I was running my own label," he told *Black Beauty*.) Ironically, it was *Entertainment Weekly*, a so-called "white" magazine, that dared to expose him: "Oakland rapper Too $hort seems to be operating on mental cruise control as he recounts gratuitous tales of life as a player in the streets and bedrooms of his hometown."

"I'm gonna be the first to tell you that *Get In Where You Fit In* just went platinum," he told the host, again using large sales figures to compensate for his obvious shortcomings. Then he lapsed into another self-serving anecdote. There was a rapper called Father Dom, who had released an album but had grown disillusioned with his label. "I heard that he was thinking about giving up music and got his phone number," the Good Samaritan $hort said; "called him up and told him to come with us."

Cautiously arriving at producer Ant Banks' studio, Dom unveiled a few of his own ideas. Banks heard the concepts then said, "Aw, that's fake." During the argument that followed, according to $hort, Dom went for a stick and Banks lifted him by the collar.

"Banks is an instigator," $hort shrugged.

▼

Goldie was wearing gold slacks, matching dress shirt, black suede shoes and a corny pimp derby, but still he seemed nervous. He sat on his stool with his chin in his chest and looked up only when the host directed a question towards him. Finally! A chance to promote his new album! The twinkle in his eyes fizzled when $hort answered for him. $hort had discovered his entourage, given them their break, and they could bask in the limelight as long as they didn't overshadow their benefactor.

"Why don't you tell him about your lyrics," $hort said, tapping Goldie's knee—a signal that he could now speak. The tense-faced Dangerous Crew struggled to appear relaxed. $hort was friendly and would gladly give the shirt off his back—to keep them loyal and dependent—but he was also as demanding as James Brown or Prince. In fact, this charade evoked the short film Prince sent to the media during his *Purple Rain* heyday. His cowardly bandmates pretended to listen as he rambled on about James Brown concerts.

Members of the Dangerous Crew spoke their minds but always with $hort glancing over with quivering lips, ready to leap in at any minute, should unflattering topics arise. A precocious seven-year-old named Baby D, who appeared on $hort's album, performed a short freestyle. Everyone laughed and said, "Isn't he cute?" while $hort handed him a twenty-dollar bill and steered him towards a woman offstage. The woman stooped to hear his tiny voice. "This is from $hort," he told her. "He wants you to buy him some chicken." From the set, $hort raised his neck, and with watery, pleading eyes, yelled, "Make it spicy! Some KFC!"

VI

Later that night, he was standing onstage in a smoky, loud strip club named Players, facing his protégé Goldie, and an audience of hysterical southern perverts. "Sorry to let 'em know like this, Goldie," he laughed, "but you used to be a pimp and shit!" Goldie couldn't imagine that this would be happening as he sat in his shiny ride in Sports-car City earlier that bright-skied day. He was parked behind an automotive accessories shop that housed the studio where Erick Sermon recorded music and filmed videos.

$hort had left the Clark campus in a huff; this would be his next stop, he said. Terence's car trailed $hort's Jeep. One or two red lights later, it had gained a significant lead. It became a car chase as heated as the LAPD's with the white Bronco.

Gangsta: Merchandising the Rhymes of Violence

Terence also enjoyed that Heavy D album, continuously rewinding the increasingly annoying "Black Coffee" anthem. Outside, on elutriated streets, Christmas music was the soundtrack; everyone seemed to be rushing home with their shopping bags. This was a schizophrenic county: rural and metropolitan and populated by two distinct classes of people, lower-income Blacks and wealthier whites.

I began to regret drinking this morning's 40s, slumped in my seat and didn't care if I lived or died. Hotel rooms were miserable; the liquor cabinets were always locked; I drank too much and called forgotten friends late at night. So many people had died, I remembered; and the television teemed with holiday specials.

I caught up to Goldie as he sat in his car munching on a sandwich, far from the mack image he portrayed for album sales. He adjusted his black brim (which looked more *Urban Cowboy* than *Superfly*), and informed me that his just-released album had already sold 60–75,000 copies. He was knowledgeable about the actual lifestyles that pimps led and vilified the poseurs. A real pimp wouldn't stoop to wearing tennis shoes, he said; a real pimp knew that the fancy clothes, big hat and car ("and you got to have your jewelry") all conformed to the fantasies that future prostitutes demanded from their surrogate father figures. A real pimp wouldn't knock his lady around. If he had any real game, he wouldn't need to. If he were successful, she'd be overwhelmed and toss the money his way.

There was a nastier element, he admitted—violent "gorilla pimps" and "Mexican pimps" who sat in nearby cars as the women worked—but he distanced himself from it, socializing instead with the upper echelon at parties and conventions held in almost every major city. A secret underworld had divided North America into markets, and millionaire pimps were expanding into Alaska and Hawaii. The rap business was small-time compared to this.

It was ironic that, for all of his boasts of being an expert at controlling women, his nickname had been coined by his dear old mom. "I was closer to her than I was to my father," he said with regret. "I tried, man," he explained. "I had a girl who was very 'beneficial' to my life." She sold her ass. "She was in my corner. I hurt when I lost her not because I liked her, but because she was so 'beneficial.'"

A woman's declaration of love fell on deaf ears.

"I can't allow myself to believe what she says." As he spoke, discerning clarity arrived. In loving himself too much, he had found sanctuary; there was danger in doing otherwise. "I seen too much dirt," he said.

After concerts, married women were among the groupies. Wedding rings did not interfere with serial intercourse. Respectable married women performing every position in the kama sutra. The next day, the women would reappear with their husbands. And in most cases, he was the concert promoter.

A woman could hurt him, he felt. He would fall victim to her charms and come to depend on her. He was "a fragile dude" who shunned emotional attachment and found consolation in materialism.

"I'm totally scarred," he confessed gradually. "I don't know what it's gonna take to heal me, man. I got a lot of pimp homies." And he thought of their sad cases: they rarely retired; many were broken men with empty pockets; many had gone insane. "A lot of them tried to live the 'American Dream,' tried to have a wife, tried to have a family, right, and for some reason or another they lost it. They were totally crushed."

Goldie finished speaking just as $hort's Jeep pulled up. I ran up to it, trying to get his attention, but he drove on by.

$hort lived a lie because it paid well. Every once in a while he abandoned the "beer and football" attitude and delivered socially relevant works like "The Ghetto," "Money in the Ghetto" and "Free," and these were the songs that found him on MTV. "Thangs Change"—on the new album—lamented worsening race relations, an epidemic of teen pregnancies and mass crack addiction. He spoke as if he were John the Baptist, and one could almost picture him draped in robes. He'd have a crown of thorns on his forehead and wander through the bushes that line most American highways. He'd yell lyrics at cars that sped by.

He was "paid real good to talk bad about a bitch," he said on the song, but missed the days when women "dressed decent" and kids respected elders. He questioned his own success ("How can I make these dirty raps / number one albums back to back"), and wished children would stop drinking; he was aware of the problems facing

Gangsta: Merchandising the Rhymes of Violence

his community but made a conscious decision to stick with the sexual themes that sold better. Sex was on HBO "late at night" and "the whole world is going crazy" and we were all "related to a crackhead" and girls were "supposed to be a virgin until they marry!" But the "positive" Too $hort surfaced only once in a while; social-consciousness didn't pay as well as performing in strip clubs and telling Neanderthals, "It's okay to slap your bee-otch if she questions your actions."

VII

When night fell in the South of the 1800s, Confederate soldiers wrapped themselves in sheets, to avoid detection when frightening freed slaves. In the 1990s, new groups of uniformed men brutalized Blacks, the police and various multicultural drug gangs.

The woods were filled with ghastly apparitions chasing the ghosts of slaves, and Ant Banks, a successful twenty-five-year-old, sat in his own shiny sports car. There was indeed "money in the ghetto" as $hort once sang, and much of it had been spent on the tracks that Ant had recorded for misogynistic rappers. Nursing a 40, he stared out of his car windshield, at a row of drunkards in front of a car shop, at the ghosts.

"That shit hurts like a motherfucker," Ant began. "It was to a point where, in Oakland, I was losing two to three homiez a month. Very last month I was there, I lost somebody real close to me." A new home had been purchased in the New Black Music mecca, and he wouldn't have to worry about the violent gangs. Now he sat in his ride, holding a 40, playing a cassette of his recent work, and he didn't care if I thought he was an alcoholic. It would serve the label right; they treated him like a second banana.

Ant was aware of his reputation—some of his friends said he was a violent drunk—and admitted that during an occasional night of boozing, he may get into little arguments, may grab someone and hold him up against a wall . . . with their feet dangling above the floor . . . "But I can't even express how I feel about certain situations," he shrugged. "I can't even get all of this shit up out of me."

He enjoyed lyrics by Method Man and Rakim but you couldn't tell from his music. He admitted that he did have it all: a nice home, pool tables, video games, new cars, production work, renown. But the

Superpimp Meets the Real World

173

fame was empty; something was missing. He wanted a family, "somebody to just love me for being me, not this 'superduper producer' or 'rapper.' Just someone to love me for just being Anthony Banks.

"See, my older sister Frieda really bought me a lot of equipment," he said proudly, "and inspired me to really get to where I am. She bought me my first digital delay and sampler! She's the reason why I really am where I am."

VIII

Todd Shaw paraded around in a pimp derby and called women whores, but the memories of his middle-class childhood were fresh in his mind. His parents loved to play the newest releases by Wilson Pickett, Sam Cooke, the Temptations and Al Green. His father was a guitarist who had attended college. "I'd hear him singing—" said Todd, aka $hort, acknowledging his primary influence.

By the age of eight, Todd was in school marching bands and teaching himself to play instruments. "My brother ain't just a motherfucker that could just rap," his older brother Wayne, a parolee, yelled. "He knows how to produce and write songs and play the shit himself! He's been doing this shit for over twenty years!" Wayne was the black sheep of the family. He had recently been released from prison. He still had the old photographs of baby Todd in his marching band, "with this drum they got him, when he had on this little paper hat and shit!"

If he hadn't seen films like *The Mack* and *Superfly*, or heard blue comedy albums by Richard Pryor, perhaps the Too $hort character would never have existed. But he did and the persona single-handedly created a new market. "See, a lot of people were just fascinated by pimps," he explained, as if this were as natural as blue skies.

"In the seventies, pimps were everywhere! In movies, on TV . . . they always had a pimp in there! I still got photos I took when I was little. I used to try to dress like a pimp and shit, with this big-ass hat that didn't look right. But I wanted to be cool like them. I learned how to pimp-walk before I could walk straight."

The Too $hort image was a cleverly researched persona as destined to succeed as former marketing student Garth Brooks's "country-western outlaw." Too $hort had served Todd well.

Gangsta: Merchandising the Rhymes of Violence

But it had been a struggle. The media had been hostile, taking him to task for the "negative image," but as his fortunes increased so had his defensiveness. His days of awkwardly trying to justify himself came to an end and he seemed to accept that he would never be viewed as a wholly legitimate artist. "Now you can print anything you like about me because I know I got the money," he began to tell writers.

IX

"See, I know a lot of guys listen to Too $hort and hear men call women 'bitch' and 'ho' and wanna be like me, but I ain't no 'Super-pimp,' like I'm all invincible and shit," he eventually told me. "I'm a normal human being and a *businessman* doing what I gotta do. These perpetrators listen to my words and wanna start calling their women 'bee-atch' but they're soft inside-out. What I try to do with my lyrics is teach them how not to be a punk in a male-female situation."

His thoughts were jumbled; he didn't know what to say. He didn't have to say anything.

"Most writers want me to speak in broken English with the slang and all that. They ride around with me in my car and see me make a few phone calls and they go back and write the same story about how I'm not really a pimp, that I'm all about business, that I'm not what I claim to be. But I never fell into the Too $hort image. The shit on wax is just make-believe. I just gotta be myself. I'm a writer. I don't force my pen into making an image. I'm just true to the pimp game. But"—he said, sounding persecuted—"I ain't putting pimps on no pedestal or telling people to go out and do that."

X

The skies were dark and I was still in Banks' car. Terence and Jamal, a young teen from Illegal, were in the backseat. We had gone through various 40s and Jamal now sparked up a blunt. I had yet to interview $hort. He told me to meet him at a certain place ("I have to pick up my car by six or I won't get it today"), then suddenly remembered another appointment. "I have to drive for thirty minutes and I'll be right back. You can wait here." An hour later, across town, he stood in front of an automotive shop, drinking beer with both members of Illegal. He suddenly remembered another appointment.

Jamal got into Banks' ride and we drove to a weed spot across town.

A Crip named Popeye Loc joined them in the backseat. Everything was cool until Popeye raised his voice and accused Jamal's bandmate Malik of being loyal to the Bloods. Malik had appeared on Snoop's *DoggyStyle* album and Death Row executive Suge Knight "was a slob," said Popeye, meaning a Blood, any self-respecting Crip's worse enemy (besides other Crips). His voice was gruff and words slurred but he was still ready to die for his convictions. And if Suge were a Blood "that means your homie's down with them!"

Jamal vehemently denied this but a brawl was slowly developing in the backseat. Banks kept out of it and raised the volume on a Father Dom track. He drowned out their ritual of slang, jive talk and posturing. There was no use arguing with this guy, Jamal discovered, so he said, "Yeah, fuck them slobs."

Popeye was like other Crips in that he had a relative in another state, and during a visit, realized that there was room for another drug ring. But after five or six months, he was bored of this mellow town. He blamed it on the women, branding them "hoes," then said he would be returning to South Central to "make some real money."

A minute later, he was play-fighting with Jamal as one would with a lifelong friend. Jamal slipped easily into the kid-brother role. Popeye appreciated this. "This little nigga crazy but he remind me of me when I was comin' up, loc!" he said, slapping Jamal's head with a fist.

"Just don't be slapping me around!" Jamal laughed. "I know how you niggas do to BGs."

The car filled with music and they began to freestyle. Popeye had musical aspirations of his own. It was the East Coast versus the West, Jamal's complexities against Popeye's war stories, but Banks didn't hear it. Thanksgiving had depressed him; he didn't know whether to go to New Orleans with $hort or have a quiet time at home with his dog.

The strip club, Players, resembled a steak house. It was a low, flat building with an awning and a parking lot. No neon, no huge signs, no posters. We entered and the cashier refused to admit Jamal. "He's too young. He can't go in!" A police officer was within earshot. He had his chest puffed out.

"What?!" Jamal exploded. "Fuck that shit!" He marched over to the giant bouncers he knew on a first-name basis. "You know I'm always in this piece! C'mon man! I ain't gon' drink!"

Gangsta: Merchandising the Rhymes of Violence

"I know! But you can't tonight! Tomorrow! Cool out, man!"

Popeye relapsed into his old behavior. He momentarily forgot that he was out of the 'hood and wanted to scrap. "This my lil' homie, dog!" he yelled at the bouncers confronting him. "How you gonna do him like that?" He had not known Jamal for more than one hour and already he was willing to die for "the homie."

"C'mon then!" he finally roared. "Fuck this place! We'll kick it in the car, cuz!"

XI

I was alone in the crowded strip club. Everywhere I looked, a naked woman shook her ass to loud music. Everyone was handing out business cards. I made it downstairs and glimpsed $hort through the crowd. Goldie was here, sat at a table, wearing sunglasses and staring into his orange juice. "And there goes Goldie!" $hort yelled from on-stage. "The man who wears the big hat for no reason!"

By the time I reached the stage, $hort had vanished. I had a flight to catch in the morning. An hour later I caught up with him. He was sipping another drink and schmoozing with flock of half-nude strippers. "I'm fittin' to do this show, then we gonna find some girls and go back to the house," he said before I could speak. "You can come with us and we'll do the interview there, alright?" I stared at him then he drifted off. It wasn't until the ungodly hour of three A.M. that he mounted the stage, stumbled around with a drink and chanted the lyrics to "Get Some Lovin'."

He shuffled his feet and said he was a mack but looked more like a project resident on Friday night who spent his paycheck on three or four 40s. He weaved like a wino with bloodshot eyes and metronomically waved his arms. The crowd wouldn't "say ho" when he commanded. They drank their liquor and gawked at the many shapely strippers. No one cared about this player's horrific views on romance—no one but the trio of local yokels dressed like the central casting version of a California gangbanger.

Like Elvis with his jumpsuits and cheeseburgers, $hort was in Superstar mode: making money out here in the "New South"; dissing the East Coast in *Vibe*; interrupting a performance to chase strippers; inviting audience members up to freestyle and seeing most outdo him;

allowing the Cali wannabes to dominate the mic while he disappeared with drink in hand.

He was in his own world, too out of it to notice that one of the strippers in the audience had stopped shaking for a dollar-waving john. In his money-fueled madness, acting out his nightmarish version of the American Dream, with speakers blasting his prerecorded vocals at him, he didn't hear her yell, "That's him?! That's Too $hort?! What's so special about him?! He's wack!"

Gangsta: Merchandising the Rhymes of Violence

Chapter 14

Poverty's Parasite

This is the Civic Center where I grew up," Kay Gee of Naughty By Nature said, entering a gymnasium, removing his jacket and running to join a game of basketball in progress. We were in East Orange, New Jersey, on a cold winter night. He self-consciously ran up and down the court, surrounded by many "friends," and you could see that he wanted us to notice his performance on the court. Clarence Mohammed, a budding young writer for the decadent *Source*, was with us, becoming slowly disillusioned with meeting the artists he idolized.

After the game, a ball player attempted to strike up a conversation with Kay Gee. "I thought you were gonna be on tour by now," he ruminated.

"Nah, not yet," the curt reply.

The fan caught the hint and discreetly left, but reappeared a second later holding photographs and a pen. "Hey, Kay, make that for my girl and this one here for my daughter." When he invited Kay over for dinner one evening, his tone implied that he would gladly hand over his wife, if asked to do so. "We could drink some brew or something!"—as if Kay were an old long-lost buddy.

"Naw, I don't drink." His face was grim as a hatchet, and he signed his name as if stabbing the photo with his pen. The fan was in mid-sentence when Kay pushed the photo and pen back into his hands and ran back onto the court. The fan was puzzled, bewildered even, but gradually accepted that Kay wanted nothing to do with him.

There he was on the court, rejoining the game, leaping up to shoot a three-pointer.

Outside of the Civic Center, the streets were empty and quiet save for the noise made by a passing mob of youth. They were all dressed in the Naughty By Nature style. You could tell they'd been watching too many music videos. Mohammed, close to their age, puffed on a Newport and blew gray ribbons of smoke at the empty sky. "He was kind of arrogant when he signed that picture," he observed, his eyes verging on outright antagonism, his idealism about hip-hop crushed under Kay's boot, his lack of goodwill. "Yeah, that's how it goes," I responded, turning from him and staring out at the barren streets.

"He took us here just so we could go write a story about 'Rap Star still kicks it with the Poor Folks,' " Mohammed continued, standing with me on that cold empty corner, his words louder due to the general silence. There was a store across the street, I noted, then wordlessly lit my own Newport. I didn't feel up to explaining that this was standard procedure in any hip-hop interview. The artist would expect a flattering portrait that would increase album sales. They were never anything like the image promoted in big-budget videos. Some of them needed to grow up. Crow's-feet began to show around their eyes and some showed the first signs of graying hair and yet they were still "angry young men."

This lousy assignment started sometime before January 17, 1995. David Mays, publisher of *The Source*, asked me to cover Naughty By Nature's video shoot in California, but menacing floods put a stop to that. The interview was then rescheduled. "You could do it in Jersey and try to spend as much time as you can with them," he said. Mays was like every other publisher in the business: one hand washes the other. An overwhelmingly positive Naughty By Nature story equals more ad revenue for a failing magazine. This would be my last story for *The Source*, I told myself. There was a four-year relationship but it had soured. The original editors, once my friends, had walked off and a new squad of scabs had been hired. The thrill of competition was gone; there was no longer any greatness. By simply appearing in print, I bested the replacements. It was time to move on to the world of books, I sadly told myself. The pleasant days of hip-hop as a culture had ended; I could no longer delude myself; I could no longer

Gangsta: Merchandising the Rhymes of Violence

ignore that major labels had destroyed this music and controlled its direction.

We had first arrived in the vicinity of their North 18th Street block about an hour ago and it was a terrible night: the streets were dark as midnight; bands of teens claimed especial corners; others stood sentinel around brightly lit liquor stores. North 18th was lined with two-story homes and dying trees. It was silent and desolate; a dead end. The houses looked abandoned.

A Black teen in a bulky jacket floated silently out of one house like an assassin. Others followed and discreetly positioned themselves around us like bodyguards. "W'sup," said Kay Gee, emerging as grim as a wraith.

A wide-faced kid named Diesel approached. He was stocky and bundled in a black jacket, dressed like his brother Treach, who had handed his group the Rottin Raskals their recording contract. Nobody paid their dues anymore. We disagreed with his approach to songwriting—every song needed a strong recognizable hook, he demanded—and his voice filled with menace.

"You can't define hip-hop," Kay Gee interjected, his eyes like silver coins. His mouth exhaled cold mist; his tone tried to sound casual. Diesel listened, nodding at the end of every sentence. His eyes were fixed. He was in a trance, as if hypnotized. In fact, everyone was. Kay Gee was their own personal E. F. Hutton, a strong-willed type who demonstrated that he had the formula for financial success. These younger artists were like a cult. They all wore similar hoods and braids, like it was a uniform.

It was always about the pop charts with these limousine rebels. They were always "from the streets" until they sampled their first champagne. Kay Gee had made his fortune by providing crossover (white) listeners with hedonistic party themes and smoothed-out music. To hear *him* tell it, his group was the last to release hardcore hip-hop.

After the Newports were long gone, and after crossing the street, entering the store and discovering that they did not sell beer, we realized that there was nothing else to do but return to the Civic Center and rejoin Kay. He was unpleasant and a bit arrogant. We returned just as he was winding down the game and zippering up his black Adidas jacket. He didn't greet us. He was self-involved, focusing on whether the black bandanna on his head were tied in Crip or Blood fashion. He finished preparing himself for the outside world and asked us, "You ready?" Then breezed past, leading us to his '94 Montero Jeep. The Mitsubishi Montero was an unfriendly looking piece of work that seated seven, mastered all terrain, and cost about $30,000.

We anticipated a frantic cruise through agitated areas, some sort of visual proof that Kay and his group did indeed frequent nastier sections of town, but we encountered nothing but unruffled streets filled with gift shops, Laundromats, diners, banks and bus stops.

One home was as stately as the White House. I pointed it out for Mohammed, who had trouble seeing past the trees, hedges and numerous cars in the driveway. Windows were filled with the warm glow of lamps; the air resonated with the sound of mellow music turned up too high or the hum of television sets. I remembered Frank Capra's early work for some reason. "This shit is kind of slow out here," Mohammed laughed. "A perfect place to raise a family!"

Kay silently navigated the Jeep through winding roads and prefatorily said, "I like Craig Mack. Craig is real humble about himself. You got to be." His tone was that of a judge handing out a life sentence. His fingers tapped buttons on a custom-made Sony stereo. Predictably, we had reached the stage where the hip-hop artist drives the journalists through town and treats them to a latest production. This song was called "True" by West Coast act the Road Dawgs. Kay was diving into the trendy G-funk sound; his face glowed in anticipation of lucrative West Coast sales. It was unremarkable, like most of his work, and we all thought so. I opened another 40, took a long drink and handed it to Mohammed. I stared out of the window and focused on the trees and neat little streets until Kay played something else. Slick Rick's "Treat Her Like a Prostitute" finally began, a reminder that hip-hop once had been fun, that we all used to pretend it was a culture and not a career opportunity. The Jeep bounced along troubled roads and turned into a wide driveway that led into darkness.

There was the large house, looming over us, the reward for disguising true intentions and serving commercial imperatives. He casually unbuckled his seat belt and flicked off the various contraptions that made driving easier and exited the vehicle. Standing in front of the Jeep, facing the house, he was no different than the hard-line com-

Gangsta: Merchandising the Rhymes of Violence

munist leaders in Russia who masterfully pledged allegiance to the poor, but kept their privileges well-hidden.

He affected a grim face as he strode across the massive lawn, passed a large eleven-bedroom work and entered a second home in progress. He really had no reason to be upset. Despite his "anger" he was able to keep peeking behind him. He wanted to ensure that, while pursuing him, we also noticed the splendor. After a quick peek inside the new residence, he turned back toward the slight hill and the large, looming mini-mansion. He didn't bother glancing at the small swimming pool near his feet. It was embossed with a Naughty By Nature logo.

In the main home, television sets were turned to different channels and fought for air superiority. An audience cheered a basketball team; a canned laugh-track for an American sitcom. Family members greeted him warmly but in passing. They continued searching through the refrigerator. Some wore Naughty By Nature T-shirts; others drank from Naughty By Nature coffee mugs.

He did not really acknowledge their existence; he breezed past, half hearing their pleas and requests, like a sovereign weary from ruling, and tumbled down a flight of stairs. In the cellar, an automatic lighting system flicked on. He plopped down on a plush modern couch and stared at a sixty-inch television screen, not uttering a word as one college basketball team stole the ball from another.

He looked as wan as he did in publicity shots, where he skulked behind his bandmates as if they were human shields. His hairstyle bordered on feminine and his eyes were nervous. "I'm in a different scenario than Vin and Treach," he said. Family members banged pots and pans upstairs and created a din expected of a dependent brood. He almost winced; they were proof that he was nothing like the "ghetto bastards" his vocalists described. He grew up in church, "with my mother and all that."

His parents and five siblings had shared a two-bedroom home. He made it sound like the Waltons. "In that situation, you don't worry about it."

Like many other hip-hop artists, he wanted me to know that his childhood had been Horatio Alger with Black characters; Dickens' ambitious young urchins; Jackie Collins' fucking-and-shopping novels sprung to life. But there had been no single parent or demoralizing poverty. He couldn't bring girls home. The home was too crowded so he had to meet girls at the Civic Center.

The former nerd scowled. Since he had not been hardened by serious tragedy and had actually spent his childhood reading comic books or fixing televisions and appliances around the home, he overcompensated with being antisocial. "I look back now and be like, 'How did we survive?'"

Viewing Charlie Ahearn's *Wild Style* led to break-dancing, deejaying, tagging up and investing in a wardrobe of sheepskin coats, personalized belt buckles, shell-toe Adidas and wide shoelaces. A high-school talent show led to a group, a demo, signing with a small-time label (Bon Ami Records) and an obscure debut album (*Independent Leaders*), of which he said, "I'm sure you heard it."

"Heard of it," I corrected.

He still owned a copy and would gladly play it. Yet another "hardcore" group had once publicized a softer image. In this case, a collegiate look heavy on soft knit sweaters, dress shoes and subtle jewelry. Treach wore tight slacks and a skipper hat and Kay Gee had his hair up in a skyscraping high-top fade.

But times and popular tastes change, he pointed out. "We went through the phase of everything. I'm not gonna front. I'm not mad at that situation back then. I had a high-top, a bunch of jewelry—" It was a small thing, not worth mentioning, not important. This had nothing to do with Naughty By Nature in 1995, when they wore hooded sweatshirts, vests and padlocked chains around their necks, and carried bats while parading through abandoned projects. This was "back in the Slick Rick–type days," he emphasized. "Niggas wore Ballys and Clarks and them 'Paco' sweaters and whatever, that *regular* b-boy stuff."

"It just changed now," he shrugged again.

We started talking about one thing and it led to my mentioning a theory of mine—that Treach's flow on "O.P.P." was similar to one Slick Rick had used on "Lick the Balls."

"I don't hear it."

"Right there on 'Lick the Balls,'" I insisted. "The exact same flow."

"That's somebody's opinion."

"Have you heard that album?"

"Yeah, man! I got the shit in my car!"

Gangsta: Merchandising the Rhymes of Violence

He spoke about their last album (*Nineteen Naughty Three*) and his voice wasn't as heated. "I don't wanna make no excuses. We were kind of rushed and we weren't really relaxed while doing it."

But then he began to speak through my questions.

"Treach has his own style of quick tongue," he protested. "A lot of time people can't understand him; a lot of times I can't understand him, but if you sit down and really dissect what Treach is saying, I guarantee it'll blow your mind!"

And Treach could master different styles.

"—and there ain't too many MCs out there that can do that!"

And he could ghostwrite for other artists.

"—and you would not know he wrote it!"

"Okay, then let's talk about Eazy-E's 'Only If You Want It.' "

Written and produced by Naughty By Nature, it appeared on Eazy's *5150* EP; it sounded like one of their outtakes. "I think that's how Eazy-E wanted to make it sound, like Treach," Kay stressed, growing tense and sibilant.

"Did Treach do it for the money?" I wondered.

"Not for the money!"

"Why did he do it for Eazy-E? Lay down his vocals—"

"Who don't lay down reference vocals when they doing a track?" He was at the top of his voice, a missionary forcing his religion on a heathen. "Eazy-E ain't hardcore?" he rejoindered.

"Yes, but the issue is, why did—"

"Niggas is from NWA! Niggaz With an Attitude! That's the hardest group! Them niggas done—"

"From what I heard, Eazy can't even go around parts of his own block."

"I'm not gonna sit here and 'dirty mack' him like that. I don't care what! Look at the type of records he made. He *portrays* a hardcore group!"

"It was kind of unexpected. Honestly, Treach sounded like *A Christmas Carol!*"

"That was just his way of doing it. You gotta ask Treach that. Make sure you ask him! You better hope he's feeling alright when you ask him too. . . ."

"Anything that happens to me will happen twofold."

"What?!"

"Twofold."

"That's some slang or something. I don't under—"

"It will happen twofold."

"Oh. To happen back to him. You don't wanna go there."

Mohammed sat up from his nap, stared at the artist and sighed. "Don't even go there," he repeated.

Gangsta: Merchandising the Rhymes of Violence

Chapter 15

Rest Easy, Eric Wright

1 9 6 4 – 1 9 9 5

∎

It was October 30, 1994, and local news and MTV had their cameras
ready. A representative from the Mayor's Office in Cleveland, Ohio,
was going to present Bones Thugs and Harmony with a plaque. This
would be "Bones Thugs and Harmony Day." Mayor Michael A.
White didn't attend the ceremony, and wouldn't attend their concert,
either, because he was out of town, the story went, but he did send
the written "proclamation," which was read aloud to the group, to
show the people of Cleveland he cared.

"I exhort all citizens to join with me in this heartfelt Welcome
Home to our nationally known rappers," it went, "and wish for them
an exciting and highly successful career." The mayor probably didn't
even know who the hell these Snoop imitators were; this may have
been a good way to get more votes and publicity: The proclamation
was read and the group listened intently. They *were* from Cleveland
but had emigrated to Los Angeles. After not securing a deal in four
months, even after Eazy-E called expressing mild interest, they returned to Ohio. They discovered that Eazy would be performing in
town, somehow became the opening act, and cornered him backstage.
After an a cappella performance, an impressed Eazy asked them,
"When y'all wanna leave?"

And here were the gangsta rappers now, mounting the stage to politely receive a wooden plaque from an authority figure, watching as—after the mayor's flunky finished reading—Eazy ("the man who heard their promise") came onstage and presented them with their double-platinum awards.

■■

When Brian Cross asked him, "What will Eazy-E be doing at forty? Eazy replied, "I don't know. I wish I had me a big company, as big as Motown, my own," he said, not content with owning Ruthless Records. "Doing everything, distribution, pressing, everything." He never imagined he'd die at thirty-one. I never imagined that, while revising chapters of this book, I'd feel compelled to offer something broader about the man. I spent years studying what others said of him, what he said to me and I still could not figure out where he was coming from.

He wanted to be all things to all people: he wanted to say, "Fuck tha police," and attend a fundraiser for President Bush; he wanted to say, "Fuck white racists," and team with Axl Rose for a song; he wanted to say, "Fuck living," and leap into business deals that would insure a brighter future.

Writing about Eazy, I find, is like searching for the real Charles Foster Kane. So many questions will remain unanswered. He died last night in a Los Angeles hospital of "full-blown AIDS."

People I speak with are still shocked.

"Yo, did you hear about Eazy?" I asked one friend.

"About the AIDS and all that? Yeah, yeah . . ." he said, as if it were no big thing.

"He died last night."

"No he didn't. . . . He did?"

His death is depressing for many reasons. He had children, for one. Now the many NWA clones will have a field day; the door is shut on a reunion.

His recent work was far from his best—I'll never forget hearing how together he had it on *100 Miles and Running*—but still, this was Eazy-E, the ultimate underdog in a field that thrived on them, a short whiny-voiced kid who had trouble delivering his raps but somehow emerged as one of the few that stood for all that was rebellious about hip-hop.

Gangsta: Merchandising the Rhymes of Violence

I wonder if he had known he was dying when he posed for *The Source's* July 1994 cover, when he sat on that low-rider with his trademark shades on and stared at the clear blue heavens above. His face looked gaunt, now that I look at the cover again, unhealthy.

When Carter Harris returned from California, he brought one of the best Eazy articles ever written. It was an excellent, revealing profile, a fair appraisal of the world-famous rapper who never wrote his own lyrics. At this point, Eazy was still consumed with rage, still brooding over Dre's insults, over Dre's solo success; he was still toting life-size cardboard photos of Dre in his Wreckin' Cru days, still attacking Dre on musical skits on the album he had delayed releasing for years, still saying things like, "Dre's claimin' he's from a place he ain't really from, a place he packed his bags and left."

It may have been hard for Eazy to accept that—as Dre said in 1992—when Dre left Ruthless, he took the sound and the platinum sales with him. While Dre's Death Row stable was selling in the millions, none of Eazy's post-NWA acts did anywhere near as well. He had signed Blood of Abraham, a Jewish rap group that delved into egghead politics and never found an audience, and HWA, a trio whose greatest assets were in their g-strings, and he had signed a motley bunch of Snoop imitators, who sang about "the thuggish, ruggish bone."

Only MC Ren's solo album, itself far from perfect, managed to maintain the aura surrounding Ruthless Records, the aura that told consumers, "This is where you come when you want that NWA flavor," and even Ren was expressing dissatisfaction with Eazy. Ren's manager at the time let slip that Ren was considering waiting out the term of his contract with Ruthless, then heading over to a label like Atlantic. Despite these tribulations, Eazy was still, as Carter Harris pointed out, on "Eazy Street." He received money from every one of the 3,000,000-plus sales of *The Chronic*, still received royalties from the two NWA albums, the NWA EP and his own *Eazy-Duz-It* album, and had twenty or so groups signed to his label, which had itself just signed a lucrative distribution deal with Relativity Records.

■■■

He had called on a winter day and told me about his life. It sounded as if time had mended the old hurts. Every Saturday afternoon, as the day wound down and night approached in Los Angeles, close to a million people were tuning in to local station 92.3, The Beat, to hear his radio show. The former Compton baller, NWA creator, label owner, multiplatinum soloist, and nigga you hate to love had been filling the airwaves with hip-hop for close to three months. "From six to nine, I host the Ruthless Radio show," he said in January 1994. "My show's more of like a street-type thing. I play everything! East Coast, West Coast, Dre, Snoop's stuff, Rage, the Dogg Pound, Death Row—whatever sounds good."

It was incredible. He seemed to actually be burying the hatchet, acknowledging that Dre's work without Eazy did have artistic merit. "But I don't play my own records," he added, anticipating my next question. "I'm not on my own dick like that. I don't give a fuck about my shit when I'm doing the show." Which was ethical.

He admitted that this latest move was a bit of a curveball to throw at fans; he had always taken a devout anti-radio stance with his group, filling songs with curses that would render them unairable. And here he was hosting a show.

"It just happened," he explained. "I approached them. I figured I wasn't getting no love from radio anyway, so either I'd get my own show or I'd buy my own station somewhere." His last album-length EP, *187 Dre Killa*, hadn't sounded so hot. He had devoted most of it to attacking Dre. The only non-Dre song on it was an upbeat, somewhat corny ditty about getting into some girl's pants. While the album's "Real Compton Gs" video received airplay, it was basically an answerback record, not enough to hold anyone's attention for long.

Eazy's days as a respected artist were over: after the atrocious collaboration with Naughty By Nature, and a lousy *5150* EP, he had put out this second "EP." While he spoke of the upcoming album ("There's gonna be like forty to sixty songs on it"), one had to wonder. Why did he keep releasing new EPs if he had "forty to sixty songs" ready to go (some of them dating back to the NWA days when E teamed with Guns N' Roses)? It sounded like he had lost confidence in the material, as if he felt it had been on the shelf a little too long, as if he did not want the press to malign the masterpiece he kept promising, as if he had run out of ideas and needed to keep the rivalry with Dre alive, so as to fill albums with responses.

Gangsta: Merchandising the Rhymes of Violence

Instead of releasing his album, as his publicist at Relativity, Kerry Cooley, kept suggesting, Eazy would always find something else to do. First he'd sign groups and put recording on hold because he had to work with these new groups; then he'd approach radio stations and ask to host a program. Then, when he had time to complete his album, as Ren was back in the fold and Bones Thugs and Harmony had sold two million records, he'd say he had no time.

At this point, the label called me at home, suggesting that *The Source* place Eazy on the cover for the April 1995 issue; *Str8* would be completed and in stores by the end of that month. Then the label would call and mention that it would again be late as Eazy wanted to work with Bones Thugs and Harmony on their second album. One wonders why there were so many delays. Sadly, now that Eazy is gone, the folks at Ruthless will probably rush the album into stores so as to capitalize on the controversy surrounding the nature of his death. This is an industry.

IV

When Eazy called me at home, he was happy to speak about the radio show. He was prepared to buy his own station, he said, evoking images of the cigar-smoking moguls from films of the thirties. KBBT (92.3, The Beat) agreed to give him a shot, and he enlisted the aid of friends like Jesse Collins, men who knew the dynamics of putting on a radio broadcast. For his pilot, his first guest was Greg Mack, formerly of KDAY, L.A.'s now-defunct 24-hour rap radio station.

"We did the show and they liked what they heard so they called us back to do another," Eazy said. With each show, his format began to develop. "So now there ain't no hard parts. Everything's smooth."

As a radio DJ, the shoe was on the other foot; instead of answering questions, he asked them. He reunited some of the KDAY mixmasters and put DJ Yella back in the public eye; he surprised listeners with special guests like Redman and Method Man, who popped in for lengthy freestyle sessions. Eazy was happy with the show and, though he was a constant traveler, built his schedule around it. When he discussed how he'd have to catch last-minute flights in order to be on the air, he made it sound like he raced through airports, leaping over luggage like O.J. in Hertz ads.

"I got my kid's birthday coming up so that's gonna be busy," he foresaw, "but the show's a priority. I do what I got to do."

Besides hosting it, he said in an excited tone, he had recently finalized a deal with Aura systems—"They make these interactive vests where kids could hit each other in the arms and chest and noise comes out." The company would produce a line of "Eazy-E's Ruthless Bass-Shaker" stereo speakers. He also played a part in a new Rap Jams video game. "They got a bunch of rappers playing basketball against each other on different courts. And I also got my own Super Nintendo game coming out but I'll tell you about that at a later time." To top it off, *Str8 from the Muthafukkin' Streets of Compton* would see release in a few months. "But I'm'a still keep doing the show. Hell yeah! So to any artists that's coming through town: everybody's invited to come on—West Coast or East Coast! Just call my office, speak to my assistant Keisha and she'll hook it up."

▼

He had a hacking cough that winter day, making me think he had either caught a cold from a change in weather or he was puffing on weed. The cough was so bad, I asked if he was okay. He said he was. Nothing to worry about. I think he said he was smoking. He was friendly and full of plans. As he spoke, my writing hand had trouble keeping up; I ended up jotting things down in shorthand.

His former bandmates had repeatedly attacked him in print and I wanted to ask about that, but before I did, he said he was happy to talk about other things for a change. He'd already been attacked in print many times by *Source* writers. They'd also called him every name in the book: making fun of his size, his lack of skill, his hair, his relationship with manager Jerry Heller, his voice. He had suffered enough, so I kept my queries on the radio show.

When he finished answering, I slipped in a question about MC Ren, about how they were getting along. He said everything was cool, that as a matter of fact, he was about to call Ren right after we finished. I asked him to give my regards. He said he would and asked if Ren had my number. I said no; he said he'd pass it to Ren, tell him to call me. I thanked him then asked exactly when he would be releasing the *Str8* album. "Soon . . . soon . . ." he answered, but there were other things to do first; the follow-up to Bones Thugs and Harmony, completing the second Ren album, the video games, the radio show, and a book he said he was going to write about NWA, a book that would tell readers about "the whole shit."

That cough was getting worse as he spoke so I advised him to take some medicine, or at least drink some tea with honey. He said he'd be okay and, before hanging up, said if I needed an interview for my book, I should simply call the office and he'd be glad to speak with me, and that if I was ever in town, I should stop in at the show. I thanked him, hung up and turned to my girl Susan, who sat at the kitchen table with a cigarette. "How'd it go?" she inquired. I smiled and said, "It went alright. He was cool. Mad cool." "See? I told you."

I had been nervous before his call, didn't think I had anything to discuss with him. But he caught me off guard, was extremely friendly, down-to-earth, no swelled head at all. I remember thinking that he sounded more humble, as if the attacks in print had somehow calmed him down. He didn't say any "way-out shit," hardly even cursed, didn't try playing the tough-guy role. He was witty, to the point, wanting to be of help. This smart man had his whole life ahead of him, I thought. He knew how to conduct business, how to make tons of money and conquer every conceivable market he could reach.

I laughed and told my girl Sue about the interview, downplaying the detail about his cough, not thinking it anything serious. "He was probably smoking a joint or something," I told her. Her face looked concerned. "They do that on the West Coast, smoke in the office. . . ." I said.

VI

He went to the doctor in early March, thinking he had asthma, and was diagnosed with AIDS. He issued a statement to the press on March 16, 1995, then married his girlfriend Tomika Wood—after she was tested, along with her daughter, and found to be HIV-negative. His former bandmates Dre and Cube put their differences aside and visited him, but they offered no comment to reporters. Snoop called the radio station and said he was praying for Eazy. Ren expressed shock and told MTV that Eazy's predicament was "one hell of a reality check."

His new wife and his mother were at his side as his condition slowly deteriorated.

His obituary was surprisingly neat: it began with the fact that he

Rest Easy, Eric Wright

died on March 26, 1995, due to complications from AIDS; he was thirty-one; born Eric Wright; with NWA, he had "brought the rawness of the inner city to the suburbs"; he didn't know he had AIDS until a few weeks ago; doctors had informed him he was in the late stages of the disease; he had said he had no idea how he contracted the disease; warned "all my homeboys and their kin" about it. "I've learned in the last week that this thing is real and it doesn't discriminate," he said. "It affects everyone."

The obituary, a short one in the *New York Daily News*, didn't mention that he had been on life support while in Cedars-Sinai Medical Center in Los Angeles. It was a short piece designed to give the basics. To them, Eazy was a "former drug dealer who claimed to have fathered seven children by six mothers. . . ." His career with NWA, and his many contributions—good and bad—were summed up in three sentences:

"NWA scored a hit in 1988 with *Straight Outta Compton*. The album's hardcore themes sold more than two million copies. The group's second album was the first hardcore rap album to top the rap charts."

This is how Eric "Eazy-E" Wright will be remembered; these will be the facts that made him noteworthy. This is all they'll need to know.